Mr Punch
and the Police

Mr Punch and the Police

by

Christopher Pulling

LONDON
BUTTERWORTHS
1964

ENGLAND:	BUTTERWORTH & CO. (PUBLISHERS) LTD. LONDON: 88 Kingsway, W.C.2
AUSTRALIA:	BUTTERWORTH & CO. (AUSTRALIA) LTD. SYDNEY: 6/8 O'Connell Street MELBOURNE: 473 Bourke Street BRISBANE: 240 Queen Street
CANADA:	BUTTERWORTH & CO. (CANADA) LTD. TORONTO: 1367 Danforth Avenue, 6
NEW ZEALAND:	BUTTERWORTH & CO. (NEW ZEALAND) LTD. WELLINGTON: 49/51 Ballance Street AUCKLAND: 35 High Street
SOUTH AFRICA:	BUTTERWORTH & CO. (SOUTH AFRICA) LTD. DURBAN: 33/35 Beach Grove

Preface

'CAN you smile?' General Sir Nevil Macready asked me, when I came over to Scotland Yard in 1919 to be interviewed before joining the Commissioner's staff. 'I found too many long faces when I came here.'

I suppose I grinned sheepishly. Anyhow, that was the beginning of my thirty-five years there, during which I served under seven different Commissioners and fourteen Home Secretaries. 'I cannot look back upon one moment when I was bored' (as Sir Patrick Hastings wrote in the introduction to his book *Cases in Court*). 'I cannot remember one day which was not tinged with some element of adventure.'

A sense of humour may not be included in the recruiting pamphlets as one of the essential qualifications for the police service, but it is certainly a useful asset. Between the wars I was an occasional contributor to *Punch*, and the idea of a history of the police as seen through the eyes of Mr Punch began to attract me a few years before I retired. I was encouraged in this by the late Ralph Straus, who left me his extensive collection of cuttings from *Punch* and other comic papers of early Victorian days; from these I was able to select the most telling cartoons up to the turn of the century, which now adorn the walls of the corridor on the Commissioner's floor of 'the Yard'. It is to his collection also that I owe certain pictures from *Judy*, *Fun*, *The Man in the Moon*, *Moonshine* and other early weeklies* which I have included in this book—though not strictly consistent with its title—where they seemed to illustrate the current point of view more appositely than the *Punch* drawings did.

This book does not purport to be either a history of *Punch*, or a comprehensive story of the police: it aims, however, to be more than a 'scissors-and-paste' collection and—with occasional digressions—to throw sidelights on the development of the British police service as seen through the eyes of the contemporary public for which *Punch* has catered for over 120 years.

That *Punch* (like most other things) is 'not like it used to be' is the inevitable complaint of disgruntled old-stagers like myself. (The young, who sometimes find our nostalgic reminiscences rather tedious, can expect in due course to meet with the same response from their own offspring.) As we grow older, we may tell ourselves that we are more tolerant and understanding; but we do take a certain pride in being 'behind the times'. And 'Whoever sets pen to paper, writes of himself, whether knowingly or not', as E. B. White says in a foreword to a volume of his essays.

---

* Beginning in the 'sixties, *Fun* and *Judy* were the two best and longest-lived rivals to *Punch*. Both went on into the early 1900's, although towards the end they degenerated to the *Ally Sloper* or *Comic Cuts* level.

Acknowledgments to all the correspondents and all the books from which I have verified some of my background facts would involve a lengthy bibliography. I must, however, make particular reference to the generous co-operation and help I have received from the proprietors of *Punch* itself, who have given me permission to reproduce drawings and to quote extracts from material of which they hold the copyright. I should also like to extend my grateful thanks to Sir Alan Herbert for freely giving me permission to quote from his *Misleading Cases*, verses and articles.

Many of the verses filled half a page or more, so that my quotations from them, or from articles, are necessarily extracts only. For this reason I have even, here and there, had to make some slight rearrangement of the sequence, for which I trust the authors will forgive me. To anyone who misses some remembered *Punch* picture in which a policeman figured, I can only say that, after scrutinising page by page every one of some 6,000 issues over the 120 years, I have had to reject six drawings for every one reproduced in this book, selecting primarily only those which form links in the story of the police.

July, 1964   CHRISTOPHER PULLING

'WHAT'S ON TODAY?'

Punch, July 26, 1939

Foreword

BY

SIR ALAN HERBERT

Mr CHRISTOPHER PULLING has contributed both to *Punch* and the Police—he spent 35 years on the staff at Scotland Yard. Here, most interestingly, he mates the important pair, who, by the way, are well-matched in years—the '*Peelers*' began in the Metropolis in 1829, *Punch* was born in 1841. He has quoted so generously from my own humble works that I wonder he should want any more words from me. Much of what he quotes, I am glad to say, is out of date. Before and after my election to Parliament in 1935 I raged against Governments, especially Home Secretaries, who were afraid to grasp such social nettles as the divorce, licensing, and betting laws, the entertainment tax, the law of libel (all these were in my first election address). Not, naturally, to everybody's satisfaction, 'something has been done' about them all. The spirit of 'DORA' (almost forgotten now) is dead: the pub is a well respected and much improved institution; and I at least no longer rail against our licensing laws. The barbarous Entertainment Tax is dead (though an odd fragment or two seem to linger in the world of radio). Mr R. A. Butler, as Home Secretary, most gallantly grasped a whole row of nettles—Betting, Licensing, Prostitution, and (behind the scenes quietly) Obscene Publications. No other Home Secretary in the present century has faced so many dragons. The bookmakers, the prostitutes, are off the streets—as everyone, including the police, desired. Knock one problem down, of course, and another pops up. Parliament, by accident, liberated Bingo, and foolishly, I think, created the all-day betting-shop. I was for the 'letter-box' (outside the bookie's office) recommended by the Royal Commission of 1933, and included in a Bill of my own (1937). The police, I seem to remember, supported this too, but a second Royal Commission (1951) turned it down, and so did Parliament. It was the same Royal Commission, by the way, which recommended the abolition of the distinction between games of skill and games of chance: so anyone worried about 'the age of Bingo' must not throw too many stones at Parliament. Right or wrong, that democratic body was out for fair play and equal chances for all the classes. At all events, the new arrangements—for pub and punter—and even prostitute?—must have made things easier for the police. I hope so, for what new and formidable troubles confront them—undermanned, as they are—elsewhere! 'Master minds' of crime—regimented defiance—stubborn marchers—and, on occasions, savage, unscrupulous mobs. It is always easy and tempting to pick holes in a police force—like the Government itself, either they do too little or too much. 'If only' we say 'they would hunt the housebreaker with the same skill and success as they chase the "car-parker"!' In the century of their birth, and for a good part of this one, the whole purpose of the police was to protect the citizen and catch the malefactor: and then he was the people's friend. But changes in life and law have made the citizen, he sometimes feels, the main malefactor—gambling, drinking, driving, walking, and especially parking, at the wrong place or the wrong time. This is understandable but unfair: the police did not invent the motor-car, that grand ingredient of ill-will, nor did they frame the laws. It is the citizen's right to throw (metaphorical) stones, now and then, but it is his duty, especially here, to take thought before he throws. One may sympathize with the frantic motorist, and others: but how often do the rest of us have to complain?

I am glad Mr Pulling has printed my war-time verses 'Thank you, policeman', and I will, if I may, add one more extract from a Misleading Case—dated 21 June 1961:

'*Mr Albert Haddock*, giving evidence, said: I am the President of the Friends of the Police.
Sir Adrian Floss (defending): What are the rules of this Society?
Mr Haddock: There is only one rule—to give aid and comfort to the police whenever that is clearly the duty of a decent citizen'.

A. P. HERBERT

A DEMOCRATIC EXCHANGE

'He was full of hot feelings about democracy.'

Mr A. P. Herbert

'Members on the Opposition side had given a lifetime to the service of democracy.'—*Mr McEntee.*

[*Punch*, May 12, 1937

Table of Contents

CHAPTER I

Introduction

A *Punch Library of Humour*, published more than fifty years ago, ran to twenty-five pocket volumes, each containing drawings and jokes on one particular subject. These did not include one on the police. Among the thousand humorous pictures selected for *A Century of Punch* (published in 1956) there were just a few in which a policeman figured —mainly in the section classified as 'The Seamy Side'. In *Mr Punch's History of Modern England*, written by Charles L. Graves in 1921, they had been mentioned only two or three times in passing. Neither Speilmann's *History of Punch* (published in 1895) nor R. G. G. Price's (published in 1957) contains a single reference to the police. This is odd, because *Punch* was concerned with the social contacts of everyday life; and pictures, articles or verses about the policeman have appeared very frequently in its pages from the start.

Punch first saw the light of day in 1841, when Peel's New Police were already twelve years old. Launched with a capital of twenty-five pounds and sold at threepence a copy,* it experienced constant financial difficulties at first; and after a year or so the two principal partners, the printer and engraver, disposed of it (and its debts) for £300 to rival printers and publishers, Bradbury and Evans, with whom Agnews, the art dealers, were later to go into partnership, so that the proprietors are now Bradbury, Agnew & Co.

As 'The London Charivari', *Punch* had aimed to be a London version of the Paris paper of that name. In its early days at any rate it was essentially a London paper, and it was many years before it took much notice of the rural police. It was for most of the nineteenth century acidly outspoken, and the political cartoons, sometimes statesman-like, often malicious, came to wield considerable influence: British governments, it has even been said, trembled at what *Punch* might say. But it had no set programme, and its targets varied over the years. Its politics (someone has written) were always amateurish. The prestige which it has had abroad as a National Institution has been as a barometer of current middle-class attitudes—social rather than political.

'The New Police' had been unpopular at first; and *Punch* (whose contributors during those early years had their ears very close to the ground) joined in the general ridicule and slanders on the conduct of the 'typical' constable. Policemen in bulk might look inhuman and official, in the days when they were marched along the streets in single file, to be dropped off to relieve at different 'points'; but if you happened to see

---

* The price remained threepence until 1917, when it was increased to sixpence, at which it stayed until 1956.

I

ROBERT, OUR FRIEND AND GUARDIAN

Mr Punch (showing a page from his family album). 'I REMEMBER YOU WHEN YOU LOOKED LIKE THIS. CONGRATULATIONS ON YOUR HUNDREDTH BIRTHDAY!'

[*Punch*, May 22, 1929

the same men sitting down with their helmets off, you realised that they were distinct individuals with very human personalities; and that is how Mr Punch's artists mostly came to see them before long.

E. V. Lucas wrote in 1925:

> 'If fear of the police is, in England, less acute than it might be, I believe that, if there is any culpability in the matter, Mr Punch's artists are greatly to blame. Ever since the days of Leech, whose policemen wore top hats, *Punch*'s army of pencils has been busy in delineating the Force with kindliness and imposing upon it a character of geniality and tolerance.'

The policeman 'type' has naturally changed with the years—from the early drawings by Leech and Doyle and Keene, through those of George Belcher and Bert Thomas, H. M. Brock and Charles Grave, to the more modern draughtsmen such as Fougasse, Ridgewell, Gilchik, David Langdon, Douglas, Sprod and Norman Mansbridge. Up to the 'nineties every picture had to be cut out by hand on wood blocks: the introduction then of photographic processing on metal blocks accounts for a change in the general appearance of the pictures.

For more than thirty years policemen wore the tall hat: it is not until the 'sixties that we see the helmet replacing it. A full-page cartoon by Raven Hill, published in 1929, the Centenary year of the Metropolitan Police, emphasises the contrast in 'the police type' in a hundred years.

If the laugh is usually against the policeman it must be because we all like showing off our contempt for authority, just as the schoolboy does of his schoolmaster—behind his back. But it is nearly always kindly fun, because we all know in our heart of hearts that what he is shown doing he has done instinctively, without regard for his personal convenience or safety, just as part of his basic duty: 'the protection of life and property'. If I seem in this book to resurrect rather a lot of denigratory views of policemen my many police friends will, I am sure, see them as I do through rose-tinted glasses, and understand that they are a necessary part of the history of the growing pains of the police service.

In a full page of drawings by Ernest H. Shepard in 1935, round some verses in which more 'Green Ways for London' were advocated, I have found one depicting a young constable with the feet of a fawn, gaily beckoning the traffic on, against a background in which a pot of flowers replaces the orange globe on top of the Belisha Beacon.

[*Punch*, March 20, 1935

[*Punch*, March 20, 1929

Punch had also had a page of Ernest H. Shepard's drawings in Paris, which included one of the policeman in argument with the taxi-driver. 'Happy Parisians', wrote E. V. Lucas in some accompanying verses, 'sit in the street/Sipping their coffee and finding life sweet . . . Watching the chauffeurs defy the police.'

One may regret that *Punch* had not been in existence in 1829, when some of the early trials of the New Police would have provided subjects for satirical comment or drawings. Quite early, for instance, the Commissioners had to issue instructions to the constables:

> 'They are forbidden to carry sticks or umbrellas in their hands when on duty.'

Drink was a temptation to which—coming as most of the first did from 'the licentious soldiery'—too many of them fell on pay day—sometimes on duty too. Examples were, of course, made of them: of one, his companions were informed that he had been

> 'Dismissed for improper conduct in knocking at the Inhabitants' doors when on duty and asking for water, in the hope of getting beer or spirits, and too often succeeding, so that he is constantly rendered incapable of doing his duty.'

Before the first winter was far advanced provision was made for them to buy gloves from a contractor in Piccadilly; but it was necessary to caution them:

> 'If they are seen lounging about with their hands in their great-coat pockets, the pockets will be taken away.'

In 1841 the Metropolitan Police District had just been extended to approximately its present boundaries—six times its original size. The more important provincial boroughs had already had their police forces for six years; the City of London Police and about half the County Constabularies had been formed a year or two. A new code of 'good rule and government' offences in the Metropolis had just been created, to be followed not many years later by similar police provisions governing all large towns: by these the ordinary citizen was brought into daily contact in the streets with the police over a much wider field than straight crime. Only six years before, the Highways Act had made the first statutory Rule of the Road by creating the offences of furious driving, riding or driving on the footway and obstruction of the highway.

Queen Victoria had been on the throne four years and had just married Albert the Good. Sir Robert Peel was Prime Minister for the second time. (It was then that he re-introduced Income Tax—which had been abolished twenty-five years before—for a limited period of four years: but, of course, it went on ever after.) Penny postage had been introduced the year before. The railways had been started twelve years, though the Great Railway Boom was still a few years ahead. Shillibeer's Omnibus had appeared on the London streets in the same year as the Metropolitan Police; Mr Hansom's 'patent safety cab' was seven years old; the 'Clarence' (the official name for the four-wheeler cab or 'growler') only a year.

Punch in 1847 had an interesting drawing of an imaginary museum of police uniforms and equipment of the period. Unfortunately no one *did* form such a museum, before the old-style uniforms, on becoming superseded, went the way of unwanted accumulations.

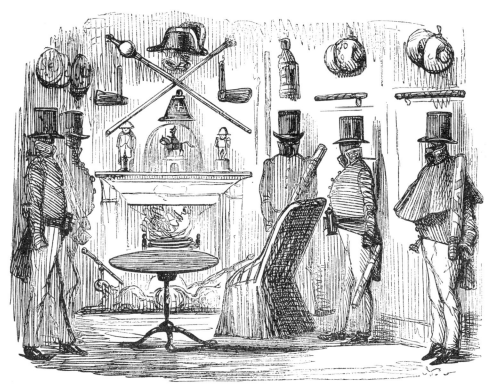

A HUNDRED YEARS HENCE.—A ROOM IN THE STYLE OF THE NINETEENTH CENTURY

[*Punch*, Vol. XII, 1847

Police museums today—those at Scotland Yard or the Police College, for instance—would give a lot to be able to lay their hands on such a collection as the illustration shows: what few relics they have laboriously collected have had to be largely reconstructed.

> 'What the armed knight of our ancestors is to us, the policeman in uniform will be to our posterity,'

the article says, and goes on to give extracts from the imaginary catalogue, which includes:

> 'The Truncheon carried by Mr Commissioner Mayne, when in attendance at the opening of Parliament. This valuable relic is supposed to have dispersed four hundred mobs by the mode in which its celebrated owner stretched it forth in moments of tumult.
> A Policeman's Cape; supposed to have been worn in four hundred different kitchens during the celebrated crusade against the larders, by which the middle of the nineteenth century was distinguished.'

Henry Mayhew (later author of *London Labour and the London Poor*) was one of the original three co-editors; but before long Mark Lemon was left as sole editor, and continued so for thirty years. He was a robust, handsome and jovial bohemian. (He had been landlord of 'The Shakespeare's Head' in Wych Street, and a not very successful dramatist; he had also a good deal to do with the launching of *The Illustrated London News* and *The Field*.) But, though *Punch* gradually became more respectable, the 'editorial conferences' were held in a hostelry or oyster bar off Drury Lane, until the mid-week Round Table Dinners (now lunches) at their own offices were founded. In the earlier years the regular contributors were paid a weekly salary—but articles or drawings had sometimes to be collected by hand from the debtors' prison, and frequently payments were already mortgaged, and had to be handed straight over to money-lenders.

It was a day when appalling puns were considered funny; and, though Mr Punch could be very serious when he felt strongly enough about anything not to give way to schoolboy facetiousness, much of the humour was by chuckles and nudges.

Thackeray began writing articles for *Punch*, illustrated by himself, when it was about three years old, and went on intermittently for ten years, signing many of them as 'Our Fat Contributor'. His 'Book of Snobs' first saw the light of day in the pages of *Punch*; and he invented 'Pleaceman X'.

Early artists included John Leech (who illustrated the Jorrocks books) and Richard Doyle (uncle of Conan Doyle of Sherlock Holmes fame, and illustrator of many of Thackeray's novels), who designed the well-known cover which continued to be used until recent times; but, being an ardent Catholic, he finally broke with *Punch* over their virulent anti-papal attitude in the 'fifties. They were succeeded by John Tenniel the cartoonist (who was to illustrate *Alice* for Lewis Carroll) and Charles Keene with many drawings of the life of the streets, in which drunks and abusive cabbies tended to predominate. Du Maurier's long run of society drawings only showed a policeman once or twice.

Shirley Brooks, who carried on as editor for a few years after Lemon's death, was a descendant of the Earl Ferrers who was the last peer to be tried by the House of Lords for murder, and to have the privilege of being hanged by a silken rope. Tom Taylor, who succeeded him, had been Secretary of the Local Government Board and art critic of *The Times*: during his editorship (1874–80) *Punch* became scholarly and heavy; but he was also a busy dramatist, whose plays included *The Ticket-of-Leave Man*.

Under F. C. Burnand, who held the chair from 1880 until 1906, *Punch* became more tolerant, abandoning invective, and the prevailing tone was one of fun and gaiety, attuned to the new middle class. He was a great clubman, and an inveterate punster, best remembered for his *Happy Thoughts*. As in Mark Lemon's time, there were frequent amateur theatricals, written, produced and acted by the *Punch* staff and contributors. He started a small Sunday riding club, which, with his habitual fondness for puns, he named 'The Two Pins' (John Gilpin and Dick Turpin). Half the members were his brethren of the Round Table, the others being fellow-members of the Garrick Club.

Nearly all the editors of *Punch* have been members of the Garrick Club; so were many of the authors and the leading cartoonists. There they fraternised with the most successful actors and lawyers. Two distinguished Scotland Yard names appear in the register of that august club—Sir Melville Macnaghten (who can be recognised as the Assistant Commissioner of the C.I.D. in Joseph Conrad's novel *The Secret Agent*, published in 1907) and Sir Basil Thomson; but only one Commissioner of Metropolitan Police—General Sir Nevil Macready, whose father, the great actor, had been one of the founders of the club in 1831. Another had been Charles Mathews the Elder, whose grandson 'Willie' Mathews was the first Director of Public Prosecutions when that office was re-created in 1908. Contemporaries have told how his private hansom-cab used to call for him at Richmond Terrace every day at one o'clock sharp to take him to the club for lunch, after which, as often as not, he would spend the afternoon at a matinée. Sir Archibald Bodkin, his successor, was also a member for over fifty years; but by his time the calls of the office were rather more exacting.

W. S. Gilbert was never a member. Offended at the refusal of some of his early 'Bab Ballads' by *Punch*, he had become the mainstay of *Fun*, their principal rival. Burnand had been librettist with Sullivan in *Cox and Box*, and never forgave Gilbert for replacing him; in consequence, *Punch* had seldom much good to say in reviewing the Gilbert and Sullivan operas. The story is told how Burnand once rather rashly remarked to Gilbert: 'All the good things are sent to *Punch*', to which he got the prompt retort: 'Then why don't you put them in your paper?'

By the 'nineties and the Edwardian era—which were relatively calm days for the police—Mr Punch had become less metropolitan in his interests. The old jeering suspicion of 'The Blue Army' or the 'Crusher' had long died down; and before the turn of the century 'Bobby' had become the friend and guardian angel of the law-abiding.

THE WILL AND THE DEED

Missus to Follower. AND YOU, YOU GREAT UGLY BEAST! GET OUT OF MY KITCHEN, AND THANK YOUR STARS THAT I DON'T TAKE YOU BY THE SCRUFF OF THE NECK AND TURN YOU OUT QUICKER THAN YOU CAME IN. G-'R-R-R!' [*Exit Follower, thanking his stars visibly*]

[*Punch*, April 11, 1877

For the next quarter of a century (1906–32) Owen Seaman was editor, and made *Punch* orthodox and polished: it would be found on most drawing-room tables in Kensington or country parsonages. There was a swing of the pendulum under his successor, E. V. Knox ('Evoe'), and in the 'thirties *Punch* began to drop the lengthy captions under the pictures embroidering and explaining the point of the joke. Hitherto it had been quite usual for writers to provide the artists with situations, fully set out, and the artists drew the pictures that roughly illustrated them. Now there may be a brief single-line legend added by the artist, or even no legend at all, leaving the readers to work it out for themselves. But it was not until 1949, when Kenneth Bird (*alias* 'Fougasse') became editor, that the object of the paper was redefined, and *Punch* took on 'the New Look'. Mr Punch had been slow to follow the influence of *The New Yorker* (which had been started in 1925). The modern cartoonist's style, simplified with bare lines and distorted or grotesque human beings, had begun to appear in the 'twenties with the drawings of just one or two artists like Bateman and Fougasse, to be followed by Pont and Paul Crump in the 'thirties; but the policeman was still more often shown kindly as a very human personality. Today character seems to be found, in a policeman or anyone else, best expressed in ungainly limbs, sharply pointed noses, ugly mouths and bulging eyes.

Dealing, as this book aims to do, with the development of the public's attitude towards the police, the arrangement is in the main chronological. But the policeman as a sort of 'Enquire Within About Anything' is timeless; and before we go back to start at the beginning it may be convenient and interesting here to select a few from the many illustrations over the years of what the constable has to put up with in the way of questions. Occasionally his patience must get nearly exhausted and he replies with mild sarcasm: George Belcher had a drawing in 1932 of the stolid policeman, asked by a tourist: 'And is the chin-strap to keep the helmet on?' replying: 'No, Lady; it's to rest the jaw after answering questions.' But the kindly understanding which he develops from his contacts, day in and day out, with all sides of human nature, makes most people ready to turn to him as a friend in need—not merely to ask the way or the proper Greenwich time, but to help solve almost any personal difficulty.

There is inevitably the female who asks anxiously: 'Oh, Constable, *have* you seen my little girl dachshund anywhere?' and the simple old lady up from the country.

Old Lady (up in London from country). 'WHICH IS THE WAY TO THE RAILWAY STATION?'

[*Punch*, August 27, 1924

In other pictures, she is asking: 'Is this the third turning on the right, Officer?' or: 'I have an idea that my niece told me to catch a one-seven-double-three-Mayfair—or is that where she lives, do you think?'

Then there is the Cup-tie Excursionist who has lost his party and asks: ' 'Ave you seen any of our lads about?' or the countryman who is alarmed at the dangers to which the policeman is exposing himself in regulating the traffic even in the days when the motor had not entirely superseded the horse.

Countryman (to policeman regulating traffic). 'Coom out o' t' way, lad. Thou'lt be run over!'

[*Punch*, Dec. 20, 1916

Occasionally too much is expected of him: in 1908 it was expert advice on the programme of a Promenade Concert.

There is the provincial visitor who blandly asks: 'Excuse me, Constable, but could you kindly direct us to London's underworld?' or the American lady who enquires: 'Say, Officer, which 'bus do I take to go an' hear an English skylark?' And there is the old lady who asks a constable, on duty in Hyde Park at Speakers' Corner, for advice as to which speaker she should listen to.

Patron of Promenade Concert (anxious for expert advice). 'Sergeant,
do you think this item is worth waiting for?'

[*Punch*, Oct. 7, 1908

'Which of these speakers would you recommend, Officer?'

[*Punch*, March 27, 1935

Preoccupied School-Teacher (vaguely noticing a hand raised). 'Yes, my boy?'

[*Punch*, Nov. 9, 1927

Sometimes perhaps the policeman misjudges the purpose of the questioner; thus one of Belcher's constables, asked by 'Abstemious Gentleman' what the time was, assures him: 'They'll be open in ten minutes.' At times he sees the town only from the police-man's point of view: to a man enquiring where Covent Garden Opera House lies the constable thinks it only necessary to say: 'Opposite Bow Street Police Station'; or to a lady visiting Canterbury who asks: 'Can you direct me to the Cathedral, please?' he replies: 'Yes, Miss. Just keep straight on till you come to a policeman, and it's just behind him.' Sometimes he takes the dignified line; thus to the young man who asks: 'Can you tell me where the Dean hangs out?' another of George Belcher's constables replies: 'The Dean doesn't 'ang out, Sir; he *resoides*.' Occasionally it is the pedestrian who misunderstands the policeman—as in J. H. Dowd's drawing of the 'Preoccupied School-Teacher'.

'I *think* THAT'S THE MAN, BUT I'M NOT *quite* SURE IF HE HAD A BEARD'

[*Punch*, March 23, 1938

The funny side of the police identification parade crops up from time to time in various forms.

'YES, THAT'S THE MAN, I'M POSITIVE'

[*Punch*, August 21, 1935

The motorist (and particularly the young woman driver) *vis-à-vis* the policeman provided the occasion for many humorous drawings—but they will fall into their own places when we come to the motor age.

The American film star who 'Thinks your policemen are wonderful' appears more

'AND NOW, BOYS, BEFORE MISS POPPY SPOTLIGHT PRESENTS THE
CUP TO THE TUG-O'-WAR TEAM SHE WISHES TO MENTION THAT
SHE SIMPLY ADORES POLICEMEN'

[*Punch*, Feb. 14, 1934

than once, also the one who, coming up against the police, takes back everything she has said, and substitutes: 'I think you London policemen are just godarned awful!'

The stolid 'Bobby' of older days was a ready butt for the humorous artist. ' "I told 'er she would be reported, your worship, to which she replied: 'Go ahead, my cheery little sunbeam' " ' gains point when you see the picture of the long-faced, rather

'AND LISTEN, BIG BOY, HERE'S ANOTHER THING YOU CAN PUT DOWN IN THAT LIL OLE BOOK OF
YOURS: "MISS LYDIA DE GRASS TAKES BACK EVERY WORD SHE SAID ABOUT YOU WUNNERFUL
LONDON POLICEMEN." '

[*Punch*, Nov. 23, 1932

dull-witted constable without a smile on his face, his eyes glued to his notebook. (It may have been the same Bright Young Person who appears in another drawing wearing her escort's helmet and smilingly telling the chairman of the bench: 'The constable said I mustn't appear before you bareheaded.')

One admires the long-suffering patience on the face of the young constable with the black eye; he has obviously had some difficulty in bringing in his burly prisoner standing in the dock beside him. 'What were you doing to allow a man of the prisoner's small physique to give you a black eye?' the magistrate is shown in another picture asking the burly constable in the witness-box; and the constable explains: 'On the morning of Toosday, the first of April, Your Worship, I was on dooty outside the "Dook of Wellington" public-'ouse, when, at the instigation of the prisoner, my attention was drawn to some-

P.C. (*referring to notes*). 'I TOLD 'ER SHE WOULD BE REPORTED, YOUR WORSHIP, TO WHICH SHE REPLIED: "GO AHEAD, MY CHEERY LITTLE SUNBEAM!"'

[*Punch*, Jan. 28, 1920

'WHAT IS THE CHARGE AGAINST THE PRISONER?'

[*Punch*, Jan. 24, 1940

thin' that wasn't there. 'E then 'it me.' In another, 'The Tough' is pictured saying to the somewhat dishevelled police constable who has brought him in to the station: 'Don't talk silly abaht you 'ad a lot o' trouble gettin' me 'ere. Why, your 'elmet's still on, an' your toonic ain't even torn.' In yet another, 'The Ruffian', about to be tackled by the policeman, says to him: 'Before I starts on yer, you'd better ring up the Police Nursin' 'Ome.'

It has been truly said that knockabout humour is based on unkind laughter at someone else's troubles. Who can help being amused at seeing a stranger slip up on a banana skin? And how much funnier it must look if he were a policeman! (Maybe the Keystone Kops used that.) To read in the papers that a policeman's own home has been burgled somehow raises a smile; a burglary at a police station or at Scotland Yard itself—as has actually happened within fairly recent years—is always good for a laugh. On Boat Race night, or Guy Fawkes night 'rags' in a university town, undergraduates used to take pride in bringing home a policeman's helmet as a trophy.

'CAN YOU LEND ME A COUPLE O' BOB, GEORGE? I'VE JUST HAD MY
POCKET PICKED.'

[*Punch*, June 17, 1914

Policemen are only human; and—for all their duties to enforce the betting and gaming Acts—are not above taking a personal interest in filling up football pool coupons or studying the odds when they are on racecourse duty. For a policeman to have had his pocket picked when on duty in uniform is definitely a joke. (It has been the lot of a Very Senior Officer in Trafalgar Square.) Some crooks have their own impish sense of humour, and it is not too difficult to pull it off in a crowd. There is an immense amount of contrasting character in the faces of the two constables in Charles Grave's drawing; and our smile has its meed of sympathy.

2

Of course, there are the standard jokes about the policeman's stock phraseology. There is the constable who, when the prisoner admits 'I did it', answers: 'Perhaps you won't mind if I write I *done* it? That is the usual expression.' And the rural constable, taking particulars of a car accident in his notebook, who asks: 'And you didn't see nobody coming round no corner. That's what you said, isn't it?' to which the superior young man replies: 'Approximately. Approximately.'

The difficulty of shaking off police habits when off duty also gives opportunities for kindly joking.

It was in 1926 that, following a press report of recent enthusiastic cultivation of Morris-dancing by the Oxfordshire police, C. L. Graves had some verses, 'Bobby and his Hobby', to the air of 'Sally in Our Alley'.

THE POLICEMAN WALKS OUT WITH HIS YOUNG LADY

[*Punch*, Nov. 4, 1931

'Of all the lads that are so smart
   There's none to match my Bobby;
He is the darling of my heart
   And dancing is his hobby.
There is no constable so keen
   In checking theft and pillage,
So large, well-nourished, trim and clean,
   And he lives in our village.
And when I meet him on his beat
   My heart goes wibbley-wobby
All for the love I bear my sweet
   Tarantulating Bobby.'

The same idea was followed in some other verses, parodying 'Coming Through the Rye', a few years later:

'Gin a bobby
Has no hobby,
He is bound to cry.'

Punch made a good deal of use of the funny remarks of pert children to their mothers. Most of these don't date much; but children can be observant. In the late 'twenties there was, for instance, the small girl, crossing the road with her mother while the P.C. is holding up traffic, who asks: 'Mother, what *did* policemen do when there weren't any motors?'; while another, sitting beside her mother in the front seat of the car, asks: 'If you run over a policeman's feet, Mummy, do you have to pay for the whole policeman?'

Small girl. 'MOTHER, WHAT *did* POLICEMEN DO WHEN THERE WEREN'T ANY MOTORS?'

[*Punch*, Aug. 31, 1937

The street urchin who comes into contact with the police has been the subject of many humorous drawings. Above all, they emphasise the complete egotism of child-hood, which A. A. Milne has summed up in a preface to his verses 'When We Were

Very Young': 'There is a natural lack of moral quality, which expresses itself, as Nature always insists on expressing herself, in an egotism entirely ruthless.'

IN THE PUBLIC EYE

'Wot's 'e follerin' the copper for?'
'It's only 'is bloomin' side. 'E wants people to fink 'e's *done* somefink!'

[*Punch*, July 13, 1910

There was a certain pride in having attracted the attention of the police, best illustrated by a drawing of G. L. Stampa's in 1910. Other pictures have shown the small boy, asked by his friend: 'Isn't that the Bobby that pinched yer fer brikin' that winder?' answering: 'That's right. I see 'e didn't get 'is promotion, after all'; or the two small boys, shrinking away as a file of policemen going on duty pass along the street, while one says: 'They must 'ave 'eard of that winder you broke.'

Lost One. 'WOT'LL I 'AVE FER TEA?'

[*Punch*, Nov. 7, 1894

There is the tragedy of the lost penny ('Will you please take particulars in your book?' one youngster asks); and the complete confidence of the child once he or she has come into police care: 'Wot'll I 'ave fer Tea?' or (the boy 'pinched' for stealing green apples): 'Got anythink at the police-station for a norrible stomach-ache?'

Small Boy. 'IF YOU PLEASE, SIR, I'VE LOST A PENNY, AND I'VE LOOKED EVERYWHERE EXCEPT UNDER YOUR FEET.'

[*Punch*, Jan. 15, 1930

J. H. Dowd made more than one drawing bringing out the self-importance of the lost boy: one is reproduced here; in another the youngster, cheerfully sucking a stick of rock, says to the constable: 'What *will* Mother do? You see, this is the first time she's lost me.' There is, of course, the modern child who, in reply to the kindly policeman's enquiry, says: 'Lost? . . . *Me*? . . . 'Op it!' But there is also the small girl who goes up to a policeman in the coronation throng and asks, hopefully: 'Please have you seen two ladies walking about without me?'

After the First World War the social status of the policeman had been raised, and books began to loom larger than boots in police work. Fifty years ago the policeman, except as a familiar figure in the streets, had little to do with the ordinary citizen: most

'SAY, COP, I LEFT HOME THIS MORNIN' AN' HAVEN'T BEEN SEEN SINCE.'

[*Punch*, Aug. 10, 1932]

of us regarded him as a stolid bulwark between us and burglars or rowdy drunks. It is the coming of the motor-car more than anything else which makes it impossible nowadays for any of us to say that we shall never find ourselves up against the police.

' "Bobbies", I call them,' E. V. Lucas wrote in 1925, 'but that is no longer current slang. Though "Bobby" has stuck, who says "Peeler" now? "Copper", too, one rarely hears. Is it possibly dislike of the term "copper" that causes all English policemen when listing property found on a prisoner to refer to pennies and half-pennies exclusively as "bronze"? Old ladies say "Constable"; wise men say "Officer"; very wise men say "Inspector". I wonder what is the status of a policeman's son: a boy with such a father should command respect, be he what he may.'

'Dum-Dum' (who was Major John Kendall) had some verses, in 1930, elaborating E. V. Lucas's theme:

'O tread that was torpid and leaden,
        O boots of a spatulate shape
Whose crunching no effort could deaden
        When warning the vile to escape,
How the music-halls rang to you nightly;
        And then what convulsions of mirth
Were aroused by remarks on a tightly
                Protuberant girth!

They came with perennial patness,
        A Joke one delighted to greet
Which had never a feeling of flatness
        Except in their feet.

But now . . .

A personage noble and nobby,
        Such dignity sits on his brow
That no-one says "peeler" or "bobby";
        We all call him "officer" now;
To a meek and subservient laity
        The gain is apparent—and yet
In the loss of some innocent gaiety
                There's food for regret.'

The volumes of *Punch* can scarcely provide a complete history of developments in the police service, but in the main only when they affected or seemed likely to interest the circles—principally Londoners—for which *Punch* catered. It was indeed often behindhand with social movements and changes, partly because it was generally apt to

'WELL, I AIN'T SAYIN' MUCH AGIN' 'IM, GEORGE, WHATEVER 'E'S DONE. 'E
CALLED ME OFFICER, WHICH SHOWS 'E KNOWS 'OW TO ADDRESS A COPPER.'

[*Punch,* Dec. 21, 1932

stonewall change, ridiculing innovations and marking time until they had established themselves.

> 'One of the advantages of a satirical magazine', writes R. G. G. Price, 'is that it can be usefully unfair. It can swing against the winner when the cause has been won, exaggerate to make its points, ignore the disease for the symptoms.'

Browsing in these old volumes, however, you find some fascinating reminders of how relatively recent are many of the things we now take for granted. In the early 'nineties, for instance, bicycling was still the latest fashionable hobby, while golf had just come south of the Border and was a 'new craze'. *Punch* took a long time to notice the kinematograph, though 'the bioscope' (not yet known as 'the movies') was by 1896 a fairly regular feature as the final turn in a music-hall programme. A few years later *Punch* was describing it as

> 'Wonderful! But it is a nightmare! . . . We had almost said, with the learned Dr Johnson, that we wished it were impossible. But to wish this is to put the clock back.'

In 1901 came bridge, the latest game, and 'ping pong' (not yet dignified with the name of 'table tennis'); and another novelty was the phonograph. In 1905 came the craze for the Kodak. In 1907 playing with a diabolo was all the rage; and there was a revival of roller-skating.

Sometimes, on the other hand, things which are nowadays accepted as commonplace were humorously forecast as wildly improbable. In 1879, for instance, there was a drawing showing Edison's Telephonoscope, 'an electric camera-obscura transmitting light as well as sound', in operation in the home—a clear anticipation of television; and two years before that the long-playing record had been foreshadowed, in a pair of drawings by du Maurier, with the explanation:

> 'By the telephone sound is converted into electricity, and then, by completing the circuit, back into sound again. Jones converts all the pretty music he hears during the season into electricity, bottles it, and puts it away into bins for his winter parties. All he has to do, when his guests arrive, is to select, uncork, and then complete the circuit.'

In 1921 *Punch* had actually had a picture of a man being shaved by an apparently petrol-driven miniature car which ran over his face: 'The auto-razor: It's bound to come!'

Punch's 'Essence of Parliament' was started in 1855, and for many years was called 'The Diary of Toby, M.P.', a title invented by Sir Henry Lucy, *Punch*'s most famous Parliamentary correspondent. In it one may find a brief and often slightly cynical

CONTROL

[*Punch*, Aug. 24, 1932

record of what transpired when police affairs aroused strong feelings in either House of Parliament.

The political cartoonists—John Tenniel, Bernard Partridge, Linley Sambourne and Raven Hill—frequently made a policeman the central figure, whether in his own capacity as a symbol of Law and Order, or in the character of John Bull, or in a cartoon of the Home Secretary of the day. Sir Herbert Samuel, for instance, is shown sponsoring the Trenchard reforms in 1932, and in 1938 Anthony Eden is shown in police uniform quoting from *The Pirates of Penzance* in relation to exchange of prisoners from the Spanish Civil War under British arbitration.

'Ah, take one consideration with another, a policeman's lot is not a happy one'

'Was there any Police Force in the world which could be described as fully satisfied?'

Sir Herbert Samuel in the Debate on the Home Office Vote

[*Punch*, May 2, 1932

Police-Sergeant Eden (to the Pirates of Cadiz):

'Yes, we are here, though hitherto concealed! So to Constabulary, pirates, yield!'

—*The Pirates of Penzance*

[*Punch*, Feb. 9, 1938

ENGLAND CARRIES ON

[*Punch*, Dec. 23, 1936

The policeman was the only human figure in the full-page drawing 'England Carries On' which appeared at Christmas 1936, when the Throne had seemed on the

THE BURGLAR'S DREAM;
OR, THE LEAGUE AS SOME WOULD LIKE TO SEE IT

[*Punch*, May 20, 1936

verge of tottering at the Abdication. In the same year a policeman was the central figure
in Bernard Partridge's full-page cartoon of the League of Nations.

But after the turn of the century *Punch* was becoming much less frank about personalities. Under Malcolm Muggeridge's editorship (1953–7) there was an increased disrespect for authority; but the fact remains that over the past fifty years there has been a marked absence in *Punch* of semi-malicious cartoons or comment on various incidents which would certainly have been used for ammunition in older days.

'The decline in the use of the proper name in *Punch*', writes R. G. G. Price, 'is due partly to the crippling effects of a law of libel whose encroachments have never been seriously opposed by the press, partly to pressure from the advertising departments not to attack advertisers, and not to puff non-advertisers.'

In consequence (as Price says elsewhere), instead of the object of the cartoon being to cause annoyance, the object became to state agreement.

Maybe the face of the Chief Commissioner of Police had begun to mean less to readers generally than it did in the nineteenth century, when cartoons of him as the personal scapegoat for every trouble were apt to appear. There was not even an allusion to 'the Chocolate Soldier' of Shaw's *Arms and the Man* when the Brigadier-General who was Commissioner in 1925 was poisoned through eating chocolates from a parcel addressed to him anonymously at Scotland Yard. Winston Churchill's presence as Home Secretary in the Sidney Street siege in 1911 had passed unnoticed by *Punch*; so did his refusal to comply with the first 'One-Way Roundabout' regulations in Parliament Square in 1925.* There was no cartoon or comment on the showing-up and downfall of Horatio Bottomley, or that of Maundy Gregory, the go-between in the sale of honours scandal of the 'twenties. (Cartoonists are not always so chivalrous about 'not kicking a man when he is down'.)

Punch virtually ignored the new Women Police for a long time, not even indulging in facetious drawings of the conflicts between the rival organisations after the First World War over what uniforms should be worn. There was nothing about the demise of the Police Minstrels after a long life. Though *Punch* had, through the pens of A.P.H. and others, hammered away at the night-club scandal, when it blew up they did not put Mrs Meyrick or Police Sergeant Goddard in the dock, as they would certainly have done forty years earlier—and had done over the 'Great Detective Scandal' of the 'eighties.

---

* He was relying on a Sessional Order, which has been passed every year since 1857, directing the Commissioner 'to see that the passages through the streets leading to the Houses of Parliament are kept free and open, so as not to hinder the passage of members'. Driving himself along Bridge Street to keep an appointment in Whitehall, he refused to obey a police constable's signal to turn left around Parliament Square, but cut across two lines of traffic, waving his Cabinet Minister's pass in the air. 'Poy' had an amusing cartoon about it in the *Evening News*, and a leader-writer in the *Morning Post* commented that Mr Churchill had crossed the political road from right to left, and from left to right, exactly as his convenience dictated, and would doubtless go on doing so. There were anxious discussions at the Home Office and in the Cabinet. Mr Churchill, however, having made his gesture, chuckled and agreed to conform in future.

Sir John Moylan in his book* says:

'The police have never escaped and are never likely to escape charges of taking bribes; but considering the temptations to which they are exposed, and how poorly they were paid in the past, occasions when we can ask with Juvenal *Quis custodiet ipsos custodes* are few and far between.'

The outstretched hand of the policeman in Linley Sambourne's drawing which appeared in November 1895 is perhaps ambiguous, and at this lapse of time it is impossible to say what were the 'certain recent cases in our Police Courts' which gave

THE EYE OF THE LAW

(*Suggested by certain recent Cases in our Police Courts*)

[*Punch*, Nov. 16, 1895

rise to it; but as it was the year in which Jabez Balfour the financial swindler had been brought back from Argentina by the untiring work of Detective Inspector Froest and

* *Scotland Yard and the Metropolitan Police*. (G. P. Putnam.) (Whitehall Series, 1929.)

sentenced to fourteen years, the fact that the truncheon weighs down all other considerations may perhaps be taken at its face value.

In the years between the wars, and since, A.P.H. (Sir Alan Herbert) was the doughtiest champion in the pages of *Punch* of the liberties of the citizen against red-tape legislation and regulations. He had begun contributing in 1910, while still at Winchester, joined the *Punch* staff in 1924, and went on writing for them all through

REHEARSING THE WESTMINSTER
PANTOMIME
[*Punch*, Dec. 8, 1937

his fifteen years in Parliament as Junior Burgess for Oxford University. Sometimes there was not all that much difference between what he said in *Punch* or in the House.

> 'Sing me the Statesman's Mind, O Muse, that I
> May know the "Wherefore" and withal the "Why",'

he had written before he was twenty.

It is in his 'Misleading Cases in the Common Law', the first of which appeared in 1924, that he touches most closely on matters which come into the everyday work of the police. Himself a barrister, he was able to preserve the legal framework of possibility in

3

the most outrageous improbabilities. R. G. G. Price sums him up as a satirist and a reformer,

SENTIMENT
[*Punch*, May 6, 1925]

'the greatest English journalist of his time. He regarded right and wrong as worth fighting about, and said in print the kind of things that people said in private'.

'Albert Haddock' must have been the most prolific litigant of all times—quite frequently in opposition to the police; but his sponsor had a real understanding and affection for the ordinary policeman—which was reciprocated. His lyric 'The Policeman's Serenade' appeared in *Punch* in 1925, and the little operetta was afterwards played in the revue *Riverside Nights* at the Lyric Theatre, Hammersmith. It is a throwback, perhaps, to the romanticised policeman of his childhood. The policeman is a rival, with the milkman and a burglar, for the affections of Susan, a kitchenmaid in the house outside which the song is sung. The stage directions run: '*Discovered, a Policeman, with Lantern, Truncheon and Service Guitar;* and he sings:

"So, good-night. Sleep sound, my pretty;
  Here till dawn I take my stand;
There are burglars in this city,
  But we have them well in hand;
And whatever fears may furrow
Other foreheads in the borough
  Nothing shall this roof surprise;
Mice and burglars both repelling,
Robert guards the sacred dwelling,
  Where his lovely Susan lies." '

Though best known for the Matrimonial Causes Act which he got through Parliament after introducing it in 1937 as a private member's Bill, he was always a ready

Mr. A. P. Herbert carries his bat
amid loud applause

[*Punch*, Aug. 4, 1937

critic of the betting and licensing laws, and any others which may not really offend against the conscience of the general public very seriously.

> 'Let's stop somebody from doing something!
>   Everybody does too much.
>
> .   .   .   .   .
>
> Let's find out what everyone is doing,
>   And then stop everyone from doing it,'

he wrote in *Ballads for Broadbrows* in 1928.

In 1936 (the year after he had entered Parliament) he drafted in verse for *Punch* the Spring (Arrangements) Bill. There is only room to print extracts from a few of the eleven Clauses with their various subsections:

> 'Subsection (i) of Section Four of any Act that seems a bore, and all the Acts concerning beer, and every Act that is not clear (always excepting Schedule A) shall be repealed and thrown away. . . . And notwithstanding any cracked provision in a previous Act, to give a constable a kiss is not felonious after this. . . . Whoever does a

ST VALENTINE'S DAY

EROS (REJUVENATED) DOES A LITTLE SNIPING

[*Punch*, Feb. 10, 1932

silly thing need only answer " 'Tis the Spring"; and this shall be a good defence in any Court with any sense. . . . It shall be deemed that everyone has come into the world for fun. This shall be printed on the wall of every office in Whitehall. . . .

'Provided that', he finishes, 'if strong objection should be expressed to any Section, that Section shall not have effect except for those who don't object.'

One of the earlier and most famous of his cases was that of *Rex* v. *Haddock* (1927)— 'Is Magna Carta Law?' In this case Haddock was appealing to the High Court against a summary conviction under the Transport and Irritation of Motorists Act, 1920, for causing an obstruction by leaving his motor-car unattended in a blind alley, though it was not disputed that no one had wanted to use it. The magistrates had, 'very properly' (to quote Mr Justice Lugg) 'brushed aside this somewhat frivolous defence', and fined Mr Haddock two pounds and costs, with additional costs of one pound for conducting his defence in rhymed couplets. Haddock based his appeal on the fourteenth chapter of Magna Carta, which is directed against excessive fines. 'In this Court', he makes Mr Justice Lugg say, delivering judgment,

'we are not concerned with private or with public life, but with the law, which has not much relation to either. Out of the thirty-seven chapters of Magna Carta, at least twenty-three have become obsolete, or have been abolished by subsequent legislation.'

He therefore dismisses the appeal, finding that Magna Carta is no longer the law. 'I am sorry to say that the Magistrate was right,' he makes the Lord Chief Justice say in dismissing another of Haddock's appeals, in 1933,

'The conviction rests upon the ancient but now, in substance, meaningless distinction between felony and misdemeanour. . . . It cannot even be said that all felonies are more repellent crimes than all misdemeanours.'

He goes on to set out, as concisely as in any legal textbook, the powers of arrest for felony or misdemeanour respectively. A few years later J. C. Squire dealt in verse in *Punch* with the equal ignorance of the ordinary citizen as to the meaning of a 'Tort'.

> 'I asked a solicitor once,
>   He calmly refused to reply;
> He could not believe such a dunce
>   Of a layman existed as I,
> When I craved for the slightest suggestion
>   Concerning the way that the Court
> Decides the bewildering question
>   Of what is and what is not a Tort.
>
> I shall go to my grave quite uncertain
>   If I've ever committed a Tort.'

'A.P.H.' was the champion of the pedestrian against the motorist, and a bitter opponent of the *agent provocateur*. There will be other quotations from his 'Misleading Cases' in Chapter IV of this book, as they come into the general story of the police. Here it is only necessary to say a little about his other great interest—the River. He had served in the Royal Naval Division at Gallipoli, has lived for over forty years by the Thames at Hammersmith, where his *Water Gipsy* has long been a familiar sight, and was a Petty Officer in the Naval Auxiliary Patrol in the last war.

In a Misleading Case in 1930 Haddock was sued for negligence for damage to a motor-car by paddling his boat along the wrong side of the road on Chiswick Mall while it was under water after a spring tide. Haddock's defence was that, the road having become part of the tideway, he had been correctly following the law of the sea— 'Port to Port'—in other words, keeping to the right instead of the left; and further that it was the duty of a steam-vessel to keep out of the way of a rowing boat. The President of the Divorce, Probate and Admiralty Division, to whom the case had been referred from the King's Bench, gave judgment in favour of Mr Haddock.

Later 'A.P.H.' was pointing out in *Punch* some of the errors commonly made by writers of crime thrillers who bring the river into their stories.

> 'How often does the great detective, in baffled search for a clue, look out thought-fully from the windows of Scotland Yard and see "the river flowing sluggishly by". Except for a few minutes near the top of the flood or the end of the ebb, the Thames flows past Scotland Yard by no means "sluggishly". It flows at two-and-a-half to three miles an hour.
>
> Far more serious and surprising are the mistakes made by the East End crooks, who have lived by the waterside all their wicked days. Even these cool hands seldom remember about the tide. . . . The tide will turn, the river will fall and expose wide spaces of mud or gravel. There in the morning will the knife or pistol lie, unless the murderer hits a patch of deep mud.
>
> The arrangements for the "getaway" by water will involve much care and cal-culation, and study of tide tables, for a launch moored as close to the banks as they usually appear is afloat for about four hours only in every twelve.
>
> Suicides too, in books, leap over the embankment walls without troubling to see if the conditions below are favourable. Instead of plunging into Paradise, he may find himself standing on his head in mud, a position uncomfortable, humiliating, but not necessarily fatal.'

I turned to the index of his autobiographical book* expecting to find many references to pages where one could hope to read his mature reflections on the police service; but all I could find was a single entry:

> 'Policemen, absence of, unimportant, in Newfoundland.'

His considered estimate of the policeman's qualities can however perhaps be found

---

* *Independent Member*, by A. P. Herbert. Methuen & Co, 1950.

best summed up in some verses he wrote for London Transport in 1944 for one of a series of posters under the general title 'Seeing it Through'. Below a head and shoulders portrait by Eric Kennington of a fine constable, there were printed these verses:

'Thank you, policemen. What would London do
Without her guides and guardians in blue?
You keep the peace, your temper, and your wits,
A dear by day, a bulwark in the blitz.

Half-way between a mother and a god,
You rule the roaring traffic with a nod:
But still have time and patience to explain
The way to Number Ninety, Lambeth Lane.

More than us all, you show the British way,
Strength without shouting, drill without display:
Pinned to your post, and longing to be gone
In different uniform—you carry on.'

'ONE OF YOUR NEIGHBOURS HAS COMPLAINED THAT YOU DON'T
KEEP YOUR DOG UNDER PROPER CONTROL.'

[*Punch*, March 1, 1939

CHAPTER II

Peel's New Police

IN his Introduction to the very first number, setting out how it is proposed to deal with different topics, Mr Punch says, under the subhead 'POLICE':

> 'This portion of the work is under the direction of an experienced nobleman—
> a regular attendant at the various offices—who from a strong attachment to "punch"
> is frequently in a position to supply exclusive reports.'

(Police 'offices' was the name given at that time to what we nowadays know as police courts.)

In the first volume there was no reference to police at all; but occasional facetious paragraphs soon began to appear, taunting them with their fondness for servant girls, and their partiality to beer. The first picture—one of several small silhouettes in a

THIS IS THE POLICEMAN MARK'D 10—LETTER Z;
WHO, ANXIOUS TO PROVE THAT THE PEACE HE MAINTAINS,
SETS TO WORK WITH HIS STAFF ON AN OLD WOMAN'S HEAD,
AND SILENCED HER BY THE LOSS OF HER BRAINS.

[*Punch*, Vol. II, p. 44, 1842

rhyming alphabet—is typical of *Punch*'s cynical view of the policeman at that date. In various casual drawings during the next few years, there was a tendency to dwell on his readiness to find any excuse for taking small boys in charge, leaving more dangerous criminals alone. An order issued by the Commissioners forbidding the police to grow whiskers led to such strong protests that it was revoked; and this was expanded into a paragraph in *Punch*.

The provincial police first appeared in a *Punch* drawing of 1st April 1843—but maybe the artist was basing his drawings on the policemen he saw in the Metropolis, not having himself been at Dover when six of the small local police force had turned out under a sergeant to form a guard of honour for the visiting Chinese Ambassador. There were still a very large number of small units of parish constables scattered over the country, where about half the counties had not yet formed their constabularies;

but since 1835 the larger towns had had
their own regular police, and there were
well over two hundred separate forces—
some of them quite tiny. Mr Punch made
several jabs at the Herne Bay force of
one man. But at Manchester—where the
Watch Committee excited his derision by
having the entire force lined up for their
new uniforms to be inspected and approved—there were already 400 men.

[*Punch*, Vol. IV, p. 136, 1843

The first 'Songs of the Police Force' appeared that year.

> 'Draw the staff, policemen, draw!
> Boldly brandish, smartly smite;
> Never fear! The pliant law
> Gives the bold policeman right.'*

But even Mr Punch recognised the growing status of the policeman. In the same
year two schoolmasters are reported as discussing the dearth of ushers ready to teach
Greek, Latin or mathematics at thirty pounds a year. 'There was no want of such
people in my time!' says one. 'My dear friend,' replies the other, 'they're all gone into
the new police!'

(The London policeman's pay then started at twenty-one shillings a week, though
two shillings were deducted for uniform and boots. Croker the diarist had written to
Peel:

> 'I find a general feeling prevailing that your policemen are not paid sufficiently.
> . . . Every artisan has five shillings a day.'

Peel replied:

> 'I have good reason for thinking that one of my police constables, if a single man,
> can find out of his pay of a guinea a week: (1) lodgings, (2) medical attendance,
> (3) very comfortable subsistence at his mess, (4) clothing; and can, after finding
> these, save out of his pay ten shillings a week.'

Those were the days!)

* Half a century later Max Beerbohm, parodying Kipling with 'Police Station Ditties', was to write:

> 'Then it's collar 'im tight,
>   In the name o' the Lawd!
> 'Ustle 'im, shake 'im till 'e's sick,
>   Wot, 'e would, would 'e? Well,
>   Then yer've got ter give 'im 'Ell,
> An' it's trunch, trunch, truncheon does the trick.'

An official advertisement in 1844 asking tenders for the supply of the police with boots led *Punch* to say:

'Policemen's boots are of two sizes only, the too small and the too large. The latter class are by far the most numerous; so that it is easy to judge a policeman by his foot, which seems about twice as big as anybody else's. These boots, or rather

'THIS IS ABOUT THE MARK, I THINK.'

[*Punch*, Vol. VII, p. 115, 1844

boats, presumably consist of leather; but they look as clumsy, awkward and inflexible, as if they were made of cast-iron. . . . The mention of the word "tender" ought to breed a kind of remorse in the breast of the Home Secretary.'

'The hat of the policeman', *Punch* was saying, 'has been compared to a chimney pot, wherefrom, however similar to it in shape and weight, it differs in the important particular of not allowing the heat and exhalations which ascend into it to escape.'

But an official proposal in 1844 to provide ventilation in the top-hat led *Punch* to publish a picture of a suggested new hat, purporting to have been designed for the police by Prince Albert himself. ('The Albert Hat' was just then the latest fashion for men.)

By the end of 1845, when the small detective branch at Scotland Yard was three years old, the deep-seated antipathy to the use of police as spies provoked a whimsical article.

THE NEW POLICE HAT

[*Punch*, Vol. VI, p. 176, 1844

'Its members, disguised in plain clothes, are now known to mix in all societies, to whose manners and peculiarities they are instructed to adapt themselves. They mingle, as exquisites, in the *salons* of fashion; they creep, as cads, into the "crib" of the costermonger. They frequent every species of tavern, from the first-rate Hotel to the Jerry-shop; and neither the freedom of the tap nor the sanctity of the parlour is safe from their intrusion.... But the evil does not stop here. In his uniform the Policeman is notorious for scraping acquaintance with servants at area-railings.... How much longer are free-born Englishmen to submit to the *espionage*, and to be victimised by the voracity of an X 10, a Y 15, or a Z 20?'

'Mr Nathan, of the Masquerade warehouse', said another paragraph a few weeks later, 'begs to inform the Commissioners that, in consequence of the prevailing practice of dressing up policemen in plain clothes, he has added to his wardrobe an extensive stock of disguises, suited to every class of society.'

And in 1847 came a brief paragraph announcing that

'a Bal Masqué on a grand scale is about to be given by the Police, for the purpose of accustoming themselves to those disguises which they are now authorised to wear on numerous occasions. . . . They can only obtain an easy bearing in their masquerade dresses by having occasional opportunities of wearing them.'

Quite frequently there are joking descriptions of novel scientific devices for the police, many of which are now in use. Traffic-lights may almost be said to have been anticipated in a brief paragraph in 1845, where is suggested

'a number of statues clothed in the official costume will be quite as useful, and far less expensive, than the present force. These statues are intended to be placed in the streets at regular distances, the same as lamp-posts; and by means of some internal mechanism will be made to ejaculate, at stated intervals, the words "Move on".'

Model of a Policeman, to be stationed at the corner
of Streets - by ringing the bell, it will spring the rattle
and bring up some of the Force! perhaps from the Areas.

The dummy policeman in the illustration from a contemporary paper carries out some at least of the functions of the police telephone-box system. (The constable whom it relieves appears to be taking time off down in the area.)

'The Detective Daguerreotype' invented by a *Punch* writer in 1847, which it was claimed would record a portrait of any thief breaking in, may yet become a reality, in these days of closed television circuits.

Electrical alarms, in the form of photo-electric cells or ultrasonic units, are now of course widely used; but more than a hundred years ago *Punch* was suggesting 'Police by Electricity':

> 'a plan for watching premises by the aid of electric sparks. . . . Instead of being regularly given in charge, the would-be burglar finds himself suddenly charged with electricity, while a somewhat milder stream of electric fluid serves to rouse the family. . . . We are not aware whether galvanic battery falls within the law relating to common assault.'

A proposal to connect all the police offices with the electrical telegraph—though another twenty years were to pass before the Commissioner could boast that it was now installed at all police stations—inspired an article in *Punch* reporting 'An Important Meeting of the Swell Mob', where one protested that science having enlisted the Levin

Brand as a Crusher, they had a new and terrible foe to contend with—they were to be nabbed through electricity, collared through the agency of magnetism. They were all for going back to the good old times, when no electric telegraphs, or police offices either, existed to restrict ingenuity and limit enterprise.

During 1847 *Punch* published a series of verses by Thackeray, 'The Loves of the New Police', narrating the romantic experiences of various policemen, mainly in the kitchens on their beats. Today these read as rather stodgy, and are too long to be quoted here. They are of interest as showing that the force which Peel had founded nearly twenty years before were still popularly known as 'The *New* Police', and still sometimes nicknamed, from the colour of their uniforms, 'Raw Lobsters' (but no longer 'The Blue Army'). It was not until the 'fifties that the names 'Cop' or 'Copper' begin to appear.

A year of revolutions in Europe, 1848, saw the climax of the Chartists' attempt to stir up revolution in England. *Punch* had not had a lot to say about the earlier scare in 1842: that had blown over after the Monster Petition had been delivered at the House of Commons by Feargus O'Connor. They had contented themselves with pointing out that over two-thirds of the three million signatories had been too uneducated to make more than their marks; and that the petition, which weighed several tons and had needed three cabs to take it there, accompanied by a procession of many thousand artisans with their wives and children, had been too big to get through the lower door of the House, and had had to be hacked to pieces. *Punch* had had a good deal of sympathy then with the malcontents, who, they said, were not malignant but impoverished and disappointed in the fruits of the First Parliamentary Reform Act.

THE MAJESTY OF THE LAW IS VINDICATED.

[*Punch*, Vol. XIV, p. 115, 1848

But in 1848 there were to be a series of demonstrations, all of which, although revolution was talked about, ended in fiascos. In preparation for a pitched battle in Trafalgar Square in March the Duke of Wellington took command of the police as well as the military, but wisely decided to keep the foot guards out of sight. The Metropolitan

LAYING DOWN THE LAW

Special Constable. 'NOW MIND, YOU KNOW—IF I KILL YOU, IT'S NOTHING; BUT IF YOU KILL ME, BY JINGO IT'S MURDER.'

[*Punch*, Vol. XIV, p. 172, 1848

Police had had a special augmentation of 500; and 170,000 special constables (of whom Prince Louis Napoleon was one) had been sworn in. Leech, who had done many humorous drawings of 'the Brook Green Militia'—formed when there was fear of French invasion a few years before—was now to make fun of these amateur policemen from all walks of life.

The declared object of the March meeting was to protest against the income tax; but Cochrane, 'The Champion of the People's Liberties', failed to turn up, after hearing that the police would treat it as an unlawful assembly. Of those who did, *Punch* pointed out that few had any practical interest in tax-paying; most of them were either ragamuffins or pickpockets, who managed to collect plenty of gold watches and silk handkerchiefs from bystanders, and then went off to break shop windows.

Mr Punch complimented them on pulling down the hoarding which, he had already been protesting, had been up far too long round Nelson's column, and only regretted that they had not touched the National Gallery, which he also disliked.

TABLEAU I

Cochranite. 'HOORAY! VEEVE LER LIBERTY!! HARM YOURSELVES!! TO THE PALIS!! DOWN WITH HEAVERYTHINK!!!!'

TABLEAU II

Cochranite. 'OH, SIR—PLEASE, SIR—IT AIN'T ME, SIR—I'M FOR "GOD SAVE THE KING" AND "RULE BRITTANNIER." BOO-HOO. OH DEAR! OH DEAR!!' (*Bursts into tears*)

[*Punch*, Vol. XIV, p. 112, 1848

Punch had two pages, reporting hour by hour on the proceedings at this meeting, as well as an interview with Lord Nelson who from the top of his column 'saw a good deal of the fun, and only wished I could have got down among 'em'.

> 'To Scotland Yard the signal ran,
> For Mayne expects that every man
> This day will be on duty.'

Early in April another large meeting was announced to take place on Kennington Common, when a quarter of a million people were expected to attend and march up to Whitehall in procession. The procession was forbidden, and Mayne rode down and interviewed the ringleader on the spot. Rain helped, and the meeting fizzled out. According to *Punch*, only a man and a boy and a dog turned up, so that Cochrane's agreement to tell the crowd to 'disperse' didn't mean much. Quoting the well-known ballad, *Punch* wrote:

> 'Mr Cochrane and his two friends may certainly say "We met", but they cannot continue by observing " 'twas in a crowd", though each of the precious trio may exclaim, in reference to Commissioner Mayne, "His eye was upon me." '

Cochrane called another meeting in Leicester Square, this time ostensibly to demonstrate against the Poor Law; but once more only a few hundred attended, mainly juveniles and thieves. A straggling procession tried several routes to Downing Street, but was turned back by the police at each. Finally Cochrane, in an open chaise, was

COCHRANE'S MONSTER MEETING

[*Punch*, Vol. XIV, p. 192, 1848

able to hand in his petition at the Home Office, but Sir George Grey, the Home Secretary, would not see him. *Punch* published a lengthy and scathing ballad 'Cockroach's Progress'. Another set of verses, 'Song of the Seditionist', includes the stanza:

> 'Should the Specials of Policemen interfere to stop our course,
> Knock them down, brave comrades—if of very much inferior force:
> If it happens that our numbers should be only ten to one,
> Let them catch us if they're able, whilst we nimbly run, boys, run.'

The cartoon 'A Great Demonstration' appeared at the end of June; and by October 'Tom Thumb at the Old Bailey' commemorated what was really the final evaporation of the threat of revolution.

A GREAT DEMONSTRATION

Mob-Orator. 'TELL ME, MINION! IS IT THE INTENTION OF YOUR PROUD MASTERS AT ALL HAZARDS TO PREVENT OUR DEMONSTRATION?'

Magistrate (blandly). 'YES, SIR.'

Mob-Orator. 'THEN KNOW, OH MYRMIDON OF THE BRUTAL WHIGS, THAT I SHALL GO HOME TO MY TEA, AND ADVISE MY COMRADES TO DO THE SAME.'

[*Punch*, Vol. XIV, p. 261, 1848

TOM THUMB AT THE OLD BAILEY

Tom Thumb (L—d R——l). 'Rebellion's dead, and now I'll go—to Breakfast.'

[*Punch*, Vol. XV, p. 163, 1848

Omnibuses and cabs—hansoms and 'Clarences' (the official name for the four-wheeler or 'growler')—were in those days a prime factor in the problem of traffic control, and naturally appear frequently in pictures of the London streets. Mr Punch's criticisms of omnibus-drivers were not always consistent: sometimes it was of the racing of rival omnibuses, sometimes it would be of their dilatoriness. Up to 1849, when fixed fares on omnibuses were first made compulsory, it had been a matter of bargaining—or bullying. He was on the side of the public against the abusive or bibulous cabby, and the rapacious conductors of omnibuses ('cads' as they were then called. The word had not yet got its present dictionary meaning of *a vulgar, offensive low fellow*, but appears in Acts of Parliament and is used by Dickens and Thackeray of conductors*).

Until a Public Carriage Branch was formed at Scotland Yard in 1850 the licensing of both vehicles and personnel had come under a Registrar of Public Carriages, being regarded mainly as a revenue matter. Daniel Whittle Harvey, the first holder of this post, had now become Commissioner of the City of London Police. Commenting on the rumour that he was using a policeman as his domestic servant, *Punch* said:

> 'On enquiry it turned out that the fellow cared little for the Harveys, but had an immense attachment to the *Whittles*.'

In the pantomime harlequinade, the policeman was always made to appear ridiculous and come off second-best; and it was being seriously suggested that the

TAKING A LEAF OUT OF THE FRENCH BOOK
THE LICENSER OF PLAYS INTERFERING WITH THE PANTOMIMES
[*Punch*, p. 273, 1851

character ought to be changed, if not cut out altogether. A drawing by Leech in 1851 shows both Clown and Pantaloon being arrested by the police, on the instructions of

* It is also the origin of the name for the golf-caddy.

the Licenser of Plays (though the latter's intervention in fact arose only because of infringements of the licensing laws which then prohibited the production of 'stage plays' at any but the monopoly theatres).

Punch had many cynical things to say about 'The Model Policeman'.

'He moves only in the most fashionable areas. . . . His heart—unlike himself—is constantly "on the beat". His taste for beauty is only equalled by his appetite for cold beef. . . . He is the terror of publicans on Saturday nights, but is easily melted with "a drop"—on the sly. . . . He is not proud, but will hold a gentleman's horse and take sixpence for it. . . . He has a vivid recollection of what another Policeman remembers.'

It was only five years since Mrs Gamp, in *Martin Chuzzlewit,* had cried:

'Where's the pelisse? If they greased their whiskers less and minded the duties which they're paid so heavy for a little more . . .'

Now *Punch* had some verses, 'Where's the Police?'

'Oh, where and oh where is the new policeman gone?
He's gone to eat cold meat with the cookmaid all alone.'

'THE POLICE ARE PARTICULARLY REQUESTED TO KEEP THEMSELVES OUT OF SIGHT.'
CERTAINLY!

[*Fun,* Oct. 25, 1862

In another issue it is suggested that every policeman should carry a label with his number on it, and should be bound to fix it on the area railings to tell where he could be found. 'Directions for finding a policeman' were:

> 'Look down every area in the street; if you do not by accident see one, ring the bell and inquire if the policeman is in the kitchen. Repeat this at every door, and you cannot fail eventually to find one.'

Such was the popular idea of the London Peeler to remain, right up to the early years of the twentieth century. Outside London, more than half the counties still had no regular constabulary. The principal boroughs, with their police forces largely modelled on the Scotland Yard pattern, were reasonably efficient; but this had the effect of driving criminals out into more rural parts, with which there was little police co-operation—indeed many of them were still dependent on unpaid parish constables. Another six years were to pass before every county was compelled to form a constabulary of its own. In 1850 *Punch* had a full-page cartoon showing 'Burglars Carousing', with a set of verses, the first of which runs:

> 'Policeman Y to booze is gone, no watch patrols the lea,
> The house that yonder stands alone invites to burglary.
> The footpad prowls on heath and fen, no crusher stops his way.
> Uprouse ye, then, my merry men, for now's your time of day.'

Doyle's drawing—one of a series of 'strip cartoons' he did in *Punch* of the Adventures of Brown, Jones and Robinson—shows Jones rescued by the police after becoming involved in a duel with a captain of Heavy Dragoons who had insulted him at a ball.

Grand Tableau! Arrival of the Police. Recovery of Jones, and seizure of the parties by the arm of the law!

[*Punch*, Vol. XIX, p. 122

Though duelling had been made unlawful in 1819, it still went on* until the Offences Against the Person Act of 1861 put a final end to it. Wimbledon Common, the site of the picture, was a favourite place; Leicester Fields or the open country where the British Museum now stands were also conveniently accessible places.

In 1849 there was a particularly brutal murder by a man and his wife, in whose kitchen the body was found buried in quicklime. Both were arrested and publicly hung in front of Horsemonger Lane Gaol. Dickens wrote to *The Times* protesting at 'the

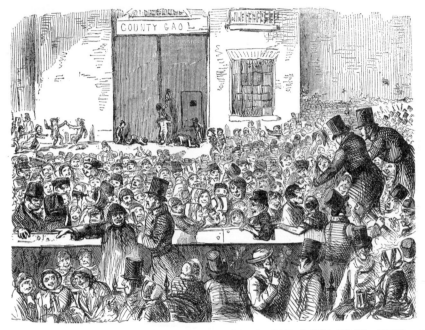

THE GREAT MORAL LESSON AT HORSEMONGER LANE GAOL, NOV. 13
[*Punch*, Vol. XVII, p. 210, 1849

wickedness and levity of the immense crowd collected at the execution'; and a drawing in *Punch* shows the difficulties of the police in controlling them. Some verses followed:

> 'Each public-house was all alight, the place just like a fair;
> Ranting, roaring, rollicking, larking everywhere,
> Boosing and carousing we passed the night away,
> And ho! to hear us curse and swear, waiting for the day.'

It is the story of My Lord Tomnoddy in *The Ingoldsby Legends* all over again. Another twenty years was to pass before public executions were abolished.

* Even Prime Ministers indulged in this method of vindicating their honour: Pitt and Canning both fought political critics; and in 1829 the Duke of Wellington called out Lord Winchelsea and had a shot at him.

The Great Exhibition naturally occupied the principal attention of *Punch* in 1850 and 1851. The Metropolitan Police were augmented by a thousand men, half of whom were required for duties inside or near the Crystal Palace (a name first given by *Punch*

Perplexed Farmer. 'YOU HAVEN'T SEEN SUCH A THING AS MY OLD WOMAN ABOUT, HAVE YOU, MR. POLICEMAN?'

[*Punch*, Sept. 20, 1862

to Paxton's vast building in Hyde Park). The rest were needed to help cope with the huge crowds of Londoners and visitors.

Punch had nothing but praise for the work of the police. Some verses printed at the close of the Exhibition included the following:

'The Great Exhibition a surplus has stored;
And surely its funds could a trifle afford,
That body to help in their age and distress,
Who did such a deal to achieve its success.

Then let a snug Station await Life's decline,
When once sturdy fists must their truncheons resign,
And e'er his worn frame is consigned to the loam,
Oh, grant the Policeman a few years of home!
    Home! Home! they've no home:
    Let worn-out Policemen have some place like home!'

Traffic control was the most serious problem for the police, especially at Hyde Park Corner. For omnibuses and cabs in particular the Great Exhibition gave full reign to the possibilities of extortion. Foreigners and provincials coming to London were at the mercy of the conductors, whose 'buses were doing such a roaring trade that back-to-back seats (known as 'knifeboards') were now introduced on the roofs of omnibuses for the first time. The humorous papers seem to have missed the opportunity of illustrating a special order which the Commissioner of Police had to issue to the force that summer:

'It was complained that persons riding and driving are prevented without cause from passing along the streets, especially at Hyde Park Corner and in the streets near the Park; also that the Police by holding out their arms to make signals frighten the horses, and that such signals are not understood.'

Within the Exhibition, at closing time in particular, the police were finding the ladies difficult to deal with.

'Nobody doubts the courage of the Police,' the text to the picture runs, 'but the gallantry of the body is being every day severely tested at the Great Exhibition. Though they would never hesitate to "clear the kitchen", they find it almost impossible to clear the Crystal Palace, when resisted by the powerful band of ladies who oppose the civil power at the point of the parasol. . . . If the regulations are really to be carried out for closing the Crystal Palace at a given hour, the only course will be to swear in a number of ladies as special constables, and throw on them the execution of the duty, which no man—with such irresistible force opposed to him—can possibly perform.'

THE LADIES AND THE POLICE. THE BATTLE OF THE CRYSTAL PALACE

[*Punch*, Vol. XX, p. 202, 1851

It was in that year that the Marble Arch was moved from the front of Buckingham Palace to its present site. A small police station was located in the top of it, and news of this inspired a fanciful drawing of its inhabitants off duty.

THE MARBLE ARCH

CLASSICAL GROUP WHICH WILL, IN ALL PROBABILITY, BE ON THE TOP OF THE MARBLE
ARCH BY THE FIRST OF MAY

[*Punch*, Vol. XX, p. 148, 1851

Towards the end of the year the pages of *Punch* were full of articles and pictures about the New Woman and 'Bloomerism'. A double-page cartoon—'Bloomeriana: A Dream' —gave sketches of women in the then improbable roles of coachmen or cab-drivers,

BLOOMERIANA. A DREAM

[*Punch*, Vol. XXI, p. 202, 1851

on sentry duty, and even as university professors; it also included perhaps the first prophetic picture of the woman policeman. (It will be observed that the men are doing the women's jobs.)

Punch's Almanac for 1853 was largely devoted to 'the Strong-Minded Woman', and contained pictures of ladies filling equally improbable roles—barrister, M.P., bandswoman at St James's Palace, and bus conductress, and—of particular interest to us—one illustrating 'The Efficiency of Female Police in what is vulgarly known as "a jolly row"'.

THE LADIES OF THE CREATION

EFFICIENCY OF FEMALE POLICE IN WHAT IS VULGARLY CALLED A 'JOLLY ROW'

[*Punch's Almanack*, 1853

Another—apparently based on the beadle in the Royal Opera Arcade—shows 'Mary protecting the Weaker Sex'.

MARY PROTECTING THE WEAKER SEX

[*Punch's Almanack*, 1853

It was about this time that the governor of Bristol Prison, obviously a keen amateur photographer, anticipating official directions, took daguerreotype portraits of the prisoners under his care—the foundation of what was later to be the famous Rogues' Gallery. Up to then, the *Police Gazette* had to depend on wood-cuts; but there were some verses in *Punch* in which 'A Gentleman of the Predatory Profession' objected to degrading the Sun itself to use 'the Collarotype' to guide the policeman.

> 'A vulgar print has just come out,
> To aid the low detective scout;
> Appealing chiefly to the eye:
> The *Illustrated Hue and Cry*.'

'A New Order of Constabulary—Scientific Detective Police' was not, as might be supposed, a foretaste of the Forensic Science Laboratories which are a part of the police organisation today, but the heading to a paragraph making fun of an article in *The Lancet* discussing food adulteration. *Punch* said:

> 'In his researches, the Detective is assisted by a microscope, which exerts a power far superior to that of the common bull's eye.'

In the summer of 1853 there was a short-lived cabmen's strike, in protest at a new Act under which the fare for the first mile was reduced from eightpence to sixpence. (Sixpenny fares were to be abolished a few years later, the minimum fare being then fixed at a shilling, which had to cover the first two miles.) *Punch* printed a 'Model Cab Act'—as the cabmen would have liked it to be—including a clause:

> 'The rate of payment to be two shillings for the first mile, and as much as the Cabman likes to charge for every mile after that.
> Ladies to be charged one-half as much again as gentlemen.'

For a few weeks, every issue of *Punch* had drawings illustrating the disputes with passengers about distances and fares, and numerous articles and verses, mainly denigrating the cabmen's attitude; but others set out the cabmen's practical grounds for grievance—the Commissioner of Police being generally named as a sort of dictator responsible for the regulations as well as the directions to his police—though he was of course only carrying out what Parliament had prescribed.* Some verses represented the cabman saying:

* That the Commissioner was not indifferent to the cabman's feelings is shown by an order issued to the force about this time:

> 'If a Cab-driver is spoken to by the Police, he is to be called "Cab-driver", and the vulgar offensive word "Cabby" is never to be used by the Police.'

'Oh cruel Richard Mayne, shabby Richard Mayne,
If I could drive you where I chose, you'd never ride again.'

There was apparently some talk of a strike in the police force: *Punch* confined its comment to a very short paragraph on 'London without a Policeman':

'We doubt if London will perceive the difference.'

The politeness of the French policeman had already been compared with the more

GOOD FORM

(You may speak to anyone in France, even to a bold Gendarme—
if you are only decently polite.)

[*Punch*, Sept. 15, 1877

laconic 'Now, Gents, move on!' of the English police constable, and Mr Punch had wondered whether it would have the same effect if he addressed an English mob:

> 'Gentlemen, I should esteem it as a personal favour if you would be kind enough to disperse, for you may not be aware that by loitering here you are greatly impeding the general circulation.'

Now Louis Napoleon (who had been a special constable in London in 1848) was considering the introduction of the English system in Paris; and *Punch* commented:

> 'Several distinguished members of our force have been dispatched from Scotland Yard to instruct the French policemen in the duties. It is not true however, as reported, that they have been accompanied either by cooks or nursery-maids.'

> 'Some may apply to the new French constable the powerful term *écraser* as equivalent to our rather expressive "crusher", and the still stronger word *écorceur* may correspond to the denomination of Peeler.'

Lord Robert Grosvenor's Sunday Observance Bill in 1855 aroused much opposition; and *Punch* had a full-page cartoon of a constable about to arrest him for working

SAUCE FOR THE GOOSE IS SAUCE FOR THE
GANDER

Policeman. 'I SAY, THIS WON'T DO. YOU MUSTN'T FOLLOW YOUR
OCCUPATION ON SUNDAY.'

[*Punch*, Vol. XXVIII, p. 247, 1854

on Sundays. On Sunday, 1st July, a demonstration by the traders in Hyde Park was swollen by roughs from all over London, and developed into a riot, in which forty-nine police were injured; and this was followed by the appointment of a Royal Commission to investigate complaints of police excesses. A picture in *Punch* illustrated the lighter side of the troubles in Hyde Park.

BATTLE OF THE HYDE PARK

GALLANT AND DARING ACT OF PRIVATE LOBBS (OF THE CRUSHERS), WHO, BY HIMSELF, STORMED AN OLD TREE, AND VERY NEARLY CAPTURED THREE SMALL BOYS.

[*Punch*, Vol. XXIX, p. 22, 1855

Punch was no respecter of personages; and in the following year a full-page cartoon shows Mr Punch himself as a policeman, cautioning the Prince Consort, whose pro-

H.R.H.F.M.P.A. AT IT AGAIN!

Policeman. 'ONLY MOVING THE PICTURES TO KENSINGTON GORE! SUPPOSE YOU LEAVE 'EM WHERE THEY ARE, EH?'

[*Punch*, July 12, 1856

posal to remove a number of pictures from the National Gallery to South Kensington had been defeated in Parliament.

Every county was now compelled to form a constabulary; but *Punch* was primarily a London journal, and it was some years still before the rural police figured in more

LATEST FROM ASCOT

Cad. 'I SAY, CRUSHER! SEEN OUR KERRIDGE?'
Inspector. 'NO, I AIN'T; BUT MINE'S JUST ROUND THE CORNER, AND I SHALL GIVE YOU A LIFT UP
to TOWN BEFORE NIGHT, I DESSAY.' [*Cads shut up, and exeunt.*

[*Punch*, June 18, 1864

than the occasional drawing. The mounted inspector pictured on Ascot Race Course may have been one of the Metropolitan officers. An Act passed in 1862 giving any

5

PIC-NICING UNDER THE NEW POACHING ACT

Rural Policeman. 'HULLO! I SAY—I SAY WHAT'S THEM BIRDS IN THAT PIE?'

[*Punch*, Sept. 13, 1862

policeman power to seize game which he had good reason to suspect had been poached, furnished occasion for a humorous drawing: even the country policeman, it will be seen, still wore the top-hat.

The garrotting scare began in 1856 and was to continue into the 'sixties. With the end of the transportation of criminals, and the lack of any system for the registration and control of convicts released on 'ticket-of-leave', the streets of London were becoming unsafe at night. Some rather lengthy verses under the title 'ELEGY, written near a Suburban Station House, by a Ticket-of-Leave man', described how the 'Crushers', deserting even their well-beloved kitchens, were snoozing in the stations, and leaving the victims of garrotters to look after themselves. *Punch* announced the launching of an Anti-Garrotte Assurance Company,

'It having become proverbial that the Police are only to be found when they are not wanted, and there being no authentic case on record of their having ever yet come up in time to prevent a garrotte robbery.'

The protective escorts which this Company would provide would be 'of such surpassing ugliness' (ran the prospectus) that there would be no danger of their finding favour in areas and 'sneaking from their duties like their leg-of-mutton-loving brethren of the

[Advertisement.]
DO YOU WISH TO AVOID BEING STRANGLED!!

IF SO, TRY OUR PATENT ANTIGAROTTE COLLAR, WHICH ENABLES GENTLEMEN TO WALK THE STREETS OF LONDON IN PERFECT SAFETY AT ALL HOURS OF THE DAY OR NIGHT.

[*Punch*, Vol. XXXI, p. 128, 1856

EFFECT OF THE ANTIGAROTTE COLLAR ON A GARROTTEER.

[*Punch*, Vol. XXXI, p. 128, 1856

Mayne force'. There is indeed a nasty suggestion in the picture that the Peeler is slinking down the steps to the area. Some rather cynical 'Rules for increasing the Inefficiency of the Police' included the following:

'Increase the number of ticket-of-leaves,
    Render prisons more comfortable,
    Make it penal for policemen to change their routes, so that the thieves and
garrottemen may safely calculate at what particular minute they will pass a certain
point',

and incidentally (a subject of considerable discontent at the time)

'Surround the "Superannuation Fund" with increasing annoyances and difficulties.'

Some verses, 'The Policeman's Tear', in 1856 saw the policeman's nose being put
out of joint by the return of the Guards from the Crimea to Knightsbridge Barracks:

'He heard the pretty housemaid read—
    "The Guards will soon be here",
    And the Peeler turned his bracelet round,
    And wiped away a tear.'

The vogue for the crinoline was giving police new problems; but during the next
few years more far-reaching matters would be occupying the public mind—the Indian

THE VOLUNTEER REVIEW

Policeman (who, we are bound to say, is extremely civil). 'WHITE TICKET, MA'AM? LETTER H!—YES, MA'AM.
QUITE RIGHT. OVER THE HURDLES, IF YOU PLEASE!'

[*Punch*, July 7, 1860

Mutiny, the Italian War of Liberation, and the American Civil War. At home there was a hotly contested Parliamentary Reform Bill on the stocks, and in the background there was constant Irish agitation. Small wonder that police received scant attention in the pages of *Punch*; though there were again many humorous drawings of recruits for the rifle volunteers, which were being formed against the fear of a French invasion.

Punch was about this time hammering away at the congestion of traffic in the streets of the City. At the time of the original establishment of the Metropolitan Police in

THE CITY POLICE

Magog. 'I SAY, BROTHER GOG, THEY SEEM TO THINK WE AIN'T NO SORT O' USE.'

[*Punch*, April 11, 1863

1829, and several times since, it had been recommended that the City Police should be incorporated in the Metropolitan; but the City Fathers had always successfully resisted. In 1863, after the failure of the City authorities to preserve order on the occasion of the passage of Princess Alexandra through the City (after her arrival from Denmark to marry the Prince of Wales), the Government introduced a Bill for the amalgamation of the two forces; but the City again defeated this attempt, and remain to this day 'a square mile entirely surrounded by Metropolitan police'.

The year 1864 saw the replacement of the swallow-tail coat by a tunic, and of the top-hat by the helmet.

'The objectionable peculiarities of the Policeman's hat', an article in *Punch* had run, 'are chiefly its extreme hardness and excessive weight, which is greatest at the crown, so that it gets instantly knocked off in a row. By night the glimmer from the silvery moon, or the refulgence of the gas-lamps, is reflected by his glazed hat-cover and enables thieves to recognise him at a distance.'

The shape of the new helmet was however to provoke much humorous comment: the cartoons show 'What Mrs Grundy says about the helmet'.

The Beer-Jug, symbolic of the servant with whom the gallant officer chats at the street corner;

The Flower-Pot, because it suggests nothing in particular;

[*Punch*, Feb. 25, 1865

The Dinner-Bell, to mark the emptiness of his head; and

The China Tea Saucer, as a hint of the shallowness of his brain.

[*Punch*, Feb. 25, 1865

Is there no feeling for Art at Scotland Yard, or is it necessary that the
Human (X 32) Form Divine be rendered hideous as well as insolent?
Who would like to be 'moved on' by such an absurdity? A noble classic
Helmet, with vizor, ear flaps, and a highly ornamental cat on top,
would have been better; or if COMMISSIONER MAYNE is really and truly
wedded to ugliness, he need not have gone further than the 'pot-board'
in his own back kitchen, the old iron saucepan is always ready to his
hand.

[*Punch*, Feb. 25, 1865

That year saw the arrest of one Franz Muller, who had committed the first train
murder—a direct result of which was the introduction of communication cords on
passenger trains. He had escaped on a sailing ship to the United States, but a detective
sergeant was sent to overtake him by steamship, and arrested him on his arrival in
New York—as Inspector Dew was to arrest Crippen, more than forty years later.
Punch had some satirical verses dealing with the German reactions to the arrest.

*A New Revised Private Police Code for the use of the executive and the assistance of the judicial
authorities* which had recently been issued to the Metropolitan police force provoked
Punch to a fanciful account of proceedings before the magistrate at Dogberry Street.

> 'The orders issued from headquarters were that the Police were not to be aggra-
> vated or obstructed, and if so treated they were at perfect liberty to lock up the
> offender,'

says the constable in the witness-box; and the magistrate, declining to allow the
prisoner to make any statement, said that

> 'he was sitting there to protect the public, and implicitly believe the word of the
> Police. Once throw any imputation on the credit of the Civil Executive power, and
> all security was at an end.'

The point is rubbed home in the full-page cartoon 'Nupkins's Justice' in *Fun*.

NUPKINS'S JUSTICE

Learned Magistrate. 'Hear the evidence for the defence? Nonsense! I won't hear a word of it!
What's the use? I could not think of doubting a policeman's word.'

[*Fun*, Oct. 13, 1866

The year 1866 saw the first roller-skating craze, and *Punch* had a drawing which showed everybody in the streets, including the policeman, skating. There were a

GENERAL ADOPTION OF THE ROLLING SKATE
LIVELY APPEARANCE OF REGENT STREET IN JUNE

[*Punch*, Feb. 17, 1866

number of drawings showing police confiscating children's iron hoops, the bowling of which in the streets was evidently becoming a nuisance.

That year was a troublous one for the now ageing and overworked Commissioner. The Reform League had been holding meetings in Trafalgar Square and elsewhere, and now threatened a huge political demonstration in Hyde Park. This was prohibited, and 3,000 police were out; but the rabble threw stones at them and pulled down the park railings and streamed into the park, and the military had to be called out for the first time to control what had become a riot. Scores of police were badly injured, including Sir Richard Mayne, the Commissioner himself, who was hit in the face by a stone. This did not prevent allegations of police brutality, but a cartoon in *Punch* gives the other side of the picture. One early result was that the police were to take over from the park-keepers the duty of keeping order in Hyde Park. But the trouble from the 'Clerkenwell Roughs' was not over. In 1868 Leaguers and Unionists were still holding disorderly meetings, and police had to seek reinforcement not only by Specials, but by men from other forces. A picture in *Punch* shows one of the latter, asked the way by a lady, explaining: 'I'm a stranger here in London, mum—only just come up from the country myself.'

RUFFIANLY POLICEMAN

ABOUT TO PERPETRATE A BRUTAL AND DASTARDLY ASSAULT ON THE PEOPLE

[*Punch*, Aug. 11, 1866

WRONG IN THE MAYNE

THE COMPLETE SUCCESS WITH WHICH SIR RICHARD CLOSED
THE PARK AGAINST ALL THE PEOPLE—WHO DIDN'T FORCE
THEIR WAY IN.

[*Fun*, Aug. 4, 1866

The Commissioner had also to shoulder the unpopularity of a dog-muzzling order, which followed an epidemic of rabies. Officialdom had persuaded itself that dogs were especially liable to hydrophobia in the height of summer—the 'Dog Days'. Responsible opinion was that cases of hydrophobia from dog bites were infrequent, but so long as

thousands of dogs were being taken up by the police as straying unmuzzled, many of
them were being and would be bitten. Many dog-lovers were writing to the Press to
point out that officials ought to know that a dog can only perspire through its tongue,
so that muzzling was particularly cruel in hot weather. Satirical articles appeared week
after week in the comic papers. *Punch* had some verses; but others on the same lines in
Fun were neater:

> '. . . Are you acting so by a
> Mistaken notion about hydrophobia?
>
> Think how a muzzle the poor helpless cur poses
> Who needs his tongue not only for the purposes
> Of respiration,
> But also—'tis the only means the tribe
> Possess—for what vulgarians describe as perspiration.'

So much criticism was there, that the order was withdrawn after a short while.
A full-page cartoon in *Punch*, 'A Change for the better', showed the constable unable
to accept refreshment being offered him by the cook at the top of the area steps, because
he was himself muzzled.

Punch seems to have missed the opportunity of humorous comment on the first
experiment with an automatic traffic signal—an apparatus erected outside the Houses
of Parliament in 1868, consisting of semaphore arms coupled with green and red
gas-lamps. It was thought very wonderful—until it blew up and injured the constable
operating it; and London had to wait more than half a century for mechanical traffic-
light signals.

In the spring of 1868 *Punch* printed a serious 'Plea for the Police', which, *mutatis
mutandis*, might have been the theme underlying the Report of the Royal Commission
on the Police nearly a hundred years later:

> 'They may fitly now be classed among our national defenders', wrote Mr Punch.
> 'For the many dangers they encounter in our service, for the weary work of ten
> hours daily watching in the streets, the wage is nineteen shillings weekly, with a hope
> by slow degrees to earn six shillings more. The man who rises to be sergeant, as not
> one in ten can do, will get eight-and-twenty shillings weekly for his work.
> '19s. a week now is not much more than equal to 14s. a week forty years ago', he
> goes on. 'The police service now requires a much higher class of men than was
> thought necessary when they started as watchmen in 1830; and the growth of the
> force has by no means kept pace with the growth of the metropolis they have to guard.
> The deduction is obvious. Not only must the force be increased, but the pay must be
> such as to induce good men to enter, and, above all, when entered, to remain in the
> service. Entering the police force should, in its pay and future rewards, be held out
> as an object of ambition to able and respectable men, and not regarded, as it is now

A CHANGE FOR THE BETTER

[*Punch*, July 18, 1868

by the most intelligent constables, as a mere resource against want, to be retained only till something better presents itself. One is not surprised to learn that the matter is becoming one of chronic discontent.'

Indeed, the possibility of a police strike was lurking in the background during these years, as a cartoon in *Judy* shows.

ROUGH ADVICE

Gentleman with bludgeon (to Policeman). 'You Strike, Old Boy. Me and My Pals, we'll support yer!'

[*Judy*, Aug. 7, 1867

The final troubles in Mayne's last year were the serious Fenian disturbances. Special Constables were again enrolled to the tune of 50,000 in London alone, after part of the wall of Clerkenwell prison had been blown down. There was much criticism of the police for failing to prevent a plot of which they had had warning; but the Home Secretary refused to accept Mayne's resignation.

Punch, like most of the press, was now constantly insinuating that it was time the seventy-nine-year-old Commissioner should retire, and criticising the force which he had moulded and controlled for forty years. *Judy* went so far as to write in November:

> 'How much longer is suffering London to put up with the aged imbecility of Sir Richard Mayne?'

More moderation was shown by papers like the *Daily Telegraph*, but even they were writing:

> 'Sir Richard has served for many years—so long, indeed, that a generous and enlightened public would gladly release him from any further exertions.'

A month later he was dead; and *Judy* published some contrite (if poor) verses 'Died in Harness', regretting many of their criticisms and paying tribute to his character.

CHAPTER III

Some Victorian Home Secretaries and Commissioners

THE Metropolitan Police Force had now grown from 3,000 to 8,000 strong; and there was considerable discussion in Parliament and the press as to what type of man should succeed as Commissioner. Mayne had been a barrister. Amongst others whose names were mentioned was Thomas Hughes, a barrister and country squire, author of *Tom Brown's School-days*, who would then have been about forty-five years old, and was later to be appointed a County Court judge. For a few months there was an inter-regnum. The new Home Secretary, Henry Bruce (later Lord Aberdare), was on the point of bringing up one of the outstanding county Chief Constables; in the end he gave the post to a soldier, Colonel Henderson, a forty-eight-year-old colonel in the R.E. who had, however, spent all but his first six years on civil duties—first as Comp-troller of convicts in the penal settlement in Western Australia, and then as Director and Surveyor-General of Prisons at the Home Office. He was to hold the post for seventeen years. There was very little of the soldier about him, though the comic papers, *Fun* in particular, were always portraying him as a military bonehead, and prophesying the militarisation of the police, whose drilling was smartened up. Threats

GUARDIANS OF THE PEACE

As they used to be in the good old times.   *As they will be if things go on as they are going.*

[*Judy*, July 20, 1870

of further Fenian outrages gave a fresh impetus to cutlass practice. (The cutlasses issued to the police had not been brought out of cold storage since the Chartist troubles of 1848.)

A Committee set up after the Hyde Park riots had now reported on the State of the Police, and there were many reforms overdue. Henderson showed his broadmindedness by giving them two days leave a month.* He also allowed them for the first time to discard their uniforms when off duty, and to grow beards and moustaches. ('A large number of the men have availed themselves of this privilege', it was officially reported.) Beards had become the fashion after the Crimean War, but moustaches had been regarded as the perquisite of crack cavalry regiments. Over the years, various orders and counter-orders about it had been issued to the police in London. They had, for instance, had standing instructions to trim whiskers so as not to conceal the number on the collar.

NEW REGULATIONS

Full-bodied Member of the Force. 'So, Bobbins, you thinks it is warming and saves trouble. Now, I likes it because it gives us a HAIR and looks MILINGTARY.'

[*Will o' the Wisp*, April 24, 1869

---

* 'One of which to be invariably on a Sunday.' There had been a brief trial of a weekly rest-day; but Henderson wrote in his Annual Report for 1869: 'It has not increased the alertness or efficiency of the police. The constable becomes unhinged and unsettled by constant interruption of duty.' Police had to wait another forty years for a statutory weekly rest-day.

Recreation rooms with improved canteens were also now provided; and this gave scope for humorous drawings. The general interest in the welfare of the policeman

INEXPLICABLE

'AND *although* THE POLICE HAVE BEEN MOST ACTIVE IN THEIR SEARCH, THE MISCREANT IS STILL AT LARGE.' (*Daily Paper*)

[*Judy*, June 17, 1868

[*Judy*, Aug. 21, 1872

led *Judy* to include, in a series of sketches of new inventions, an 'Improved Helmet for the Force'. There was also an increase in police pay, to the tune of a shilling a week. In the press this was headlined: 'Important Concession in point of pay to the Metropolitan Police', and *Punch* had a full-page cartoon of Mr Bull saying to a policeman:

'I never doubted your *Bravery*, my strong friend: what I want is more *Brains*; so, to encourage them, I'll give you *a whole shilling a week* more!!!'

Colonel Henderson quickly obtained approval for a substantial augmentation of the force, and greatly increased the numbers of detectives, who up to then had been almost as few as the original eight whom Dickens entertained at the office of *Household Words* at his 'Detective Tea-Party', and who hitherto had all been housed at headquarters. He also instituted four new posts, giving them the title of Visiting or District Superintendent,* copied from the Indian police. Of the first holders, one had come up within the force and one was an Indian police officer; for the other two he brought in ex-regular army officers. *Judy* had some verses, purporting to be spoken by a constable:

'Them Captains and them Curnels cannot give up the ideer
That they're governin' an army, in a marshal atmospheer;
But if they're so fond of solj'rin, what a pity they retired
From a service where by this time they'd have gen'ralship acquired.'

* This rank now corresponds to that of 'District Commander' in the Metropolitan Police, though it has for various periods been known as 'Chief Constable' and 'Deputy Assistant Commissioner'.

Bruce's attitude to the police was recognised as more understanding than that of some of his predecessors at the Home Office; and *Will O' the Wisp* had a full-page cartoon.

THE POLICE AT 'HOME'

Superintendent of Police. 'THIS DEPUTATION WAITS ON YOU, SIR, TO THANK YOU VERY WARMLY FOR YOUR ATTACHMENT TO THE FORCE.'
Mr. Secretary Bruce. 'YOU MAY ALWAYS RELY, GENTLEMEN, UPON MY NON-INTERFERENCE BETWEEN YOURSELVES AND THE PUBLIC.'

[*Will o' the Wisp*, Aug. 14, 1869

About this time a lot was being written in the press about the need for reform in the administration of the City of London. *Punch*, à propos of several undetected shop burglaries in the small hours of the morning in Cheapside, said:

'There is something so rotten in the state of the City Police arrangements, that people will soon begin to say that the Mansion House is as bad as the Home Office.'

Fun, however, had a humorous drawing of City policemen dancing at their annual festival, with verses which included:

'Long live our City Policemen,
Our excellent City policemen,
Poor Scotland Yard
Sighs very hard
For men like our City Policemen!'

The Metropolitan police constable probably sighed very hard, too, envying the City constable's rate of pay; for another fifty years, the City Fathers were always prepared to offer a little more to get the pick of candidates for the police.

Police boots were still a sore point.

'The stiffer, the clumsier and the tighter, the better for the pursued,' said *Punch* in an article under the heading 'New Boots for Bobby'. 'At present the policeman's boots are of such a make as to be very much the reverse of Seven League Boots. They are so made as if they had been made to order of the thieves and rogues and dangerous classes. The ends of Justice, and the protection of Society, would be furthered if those boots were all made to order of their wearers.'

It was another quarter of a century before policemen were allowed to buy their own boots, receiving a weekly allowance towards the cost.

The year 1870 was the one in which 'The Gendarmes' Duet' in an Offenbach operetta at the Philharmonic Hall, Islington—to which the Prince of Wales led all London—took the town by storm. The English version, with its catchy refrain 'We run 'em in', gave the comedians opportunities for sly digs at the Metropolitan policeman of the day; and the original gendarmes had to take seventeen encores on the opening night.

'Better-educated police' was a frequent cry in the press about this time; and *Punch* in 1871 published a picture which showed a team of three on the same job, contributing respectively the qualities of agility, physique and intellect, 'rarely to be found combined in one policeman'.

In 1872 came the first police strike, which followed a monster meeting at the Cannon Street Hotel to formulate demands for increased pay, better pensions and a reduction of the hours of day duty from nine to eight. *Fun* had a cartoon showing John Bull saying to a policeman:

'Now, my man, I don't pay any attention to these would-be military noodles! Tell *me* what's wrong, for I am quite sure you would not refuse to do duty without very sufficient reason!'

It was a hasty protest against the dismissal of a Constable who had acted as Secretary to the delegates, and was limited to three stations and 180 men, who were dismissed but, with a few exceptions, subsequently reinstated. It led however to a good deal of unpopularity with the public. In the number before Christmas 1873, *Punch* had a fairly serious article about the police.

'Recent legislation has rendered this once free nation a grievously police-ridden people. The police have been constituted a sort of prefects of public-houses. . . .

Very much has been done to place them in the same relation to the people at large
as that of beadles to little boys.'

PRO AR(E)IS ET FOCIS

Housemaid. 'O!—SO YOU MUST GO ON STRIKE, *TOO*, MR. ROBERT, MUST YOU?—LEAVIN' OF US ALL
TO BE MURDERED, LET ALONE BURGLARS? NEVER AGAIN DOWN *THIS* AREA—NEVER IN YOUR LIFE,
SIR! THERE!'   [*Locks gate, and puts the key in her pocket.*
   Voice from Below. 'NEVER AGAIN!—AS I'M A BRITISH COOK!!'

[*Punch, Nov. 30, 1872*

He goes on to suggest that, as our constables are now social soldiers, the toast at public dinners should be 'The Army, Navy and Police!'—an idea which Ronald Frankau was to repeat in a music-hall song sixty years later.

Friction between the policeman and the cab- or omnibus-driver gave subjects for

ALL'S FAIR IN LOVE AND WAR
Bus Conductor. 'WELL, BOBBY, WHAT'S YOUR FARE?'
Police Sergeant. 'BREAD AND WATER—SAME AS YOU HAD BEFORE!'

[*Judy*, Oct. 18, 1876

frequent humorous drawings. From the nature of their occupation, this was inevitable; but good-humoured if caustic back-chat came all in the day's work.

There were two *causes célèbres* in 1873—the mistaken arrest of a Mr Belt for drunkenness, and a fracas with some officers of the Life Guards outside the Argyll Rooms, when a police charge of drunkenness and assault was dismissed. Mr Punch in some rather jog-trotting verses '*Ad Robertum Misbehavientem*' cautioned Bobby, but gently:

'*Punch* has always borne in mind his Bobby's sore temptations,
As, Cooks and their cajoleries, Roughs and their aggravations;
His long-drawn hours of duty, in defiance of wind and weather,
His weary tramps, whose dust and damps tax spirits, strength, and shoe-leather.'

And before the year was out, he was to rebuke the Home Secretary, Robert Lowe, for whitewashing the police. There were some verses attached to the cartoon:

'Of whitewashing Bobby
Bob has done the job;
Wanted, now, a Bobby
Who will whitewash Bob.'

LOW(E) ART AND WHITEWASH
(*See the* HOME SECRETARY's *Defence of the British Constable.*)

[*Punch,* Dec. 27, 1873

The year 1877 brought the famous Trial of the Detectives: three of the four chief inspectors of the C.I.D. and an inspector had all got into the toils of a gang of ingenious betting swindlers whose operations extended to Scotland and the continent. Some rather

BULL'S EYE ON BOBBY

Mr Bull (*takes Policeman's lantern*). 'THANK YOU. I'LL JUST HAVE A LOOK ROUND MYSELF. STRIKES ME THE PREMISES AIN'T AS CLEAN AS THEY MIGHT BE!'

[*Punch*, Aug. 25, 1877

lengthy verses appeared opposite the cartoon, under the title '*Quis Custodiet Ipsos Custodes?*' A few couplets may be quoted.

> 'Compact 'twixt Crime and Constable? My friend,
> If there *have been* such games, those games must end.
> I'd have no French Vidocq in Bobby's shape,
> Masked in familiar helm and coat and cape,
> Nor yet a flat by the first sharp beguiled;
> Neither a Dogberry nor a Jonathan Wild.
> The Argus of the Penny Dreadful school,
> Shrunk to a vulgar cross of knave and fool!
> Consid'ring what I pay, 'twere rather hard
> Were Crime's head-centre found in Scotland Yard!'

The weekly paper *Truth* was started that year, and was for many years to be both a thorn in the flesh and at the same time of no little assistance to the police with its exposures of all forms of swindles, from bucket-shops and dud companies to fraudulent charity-mongers. Henry Labouchère, proprietor and editor, never minded appearing in the courts on charges of criminal libel, and frequently conducted his own case with great skill. No such paper as his could exist in the present conditions of the law of libel.

The whole detective organisation at Scotland Yard had meanwhile come under investigation by a Commission. A few of the Detective Branch, it came out in the official evidence, had been brought in direct from outside the force—some to contribute a better standard of education, others because they were good linguists. (Inspector Druscovitch, for instance, one of those convicted and sentenced to two years' hard labour, spoke with a foreign accent.) A cynical question paper for 'Candidates for Employment in the Detective Department' was printed in *Punch*. The following were some of a string of questions:

> 'Give a rough sketch of your coat-of-arms, and trace your pedigree for four generations. . . . Were you educated at Eton, Westminster or Winchester? Are you an Oxford Man or a Cantab? If you were not at Christchurch, Baliol [*sic*], Trinity or John's, state why you were sent to a less distinguished College. What degree did you take? Give the names of the learned Societies of which you are a Fellow. . . . Are you well up in Roman, English and International Law? . . . Give the highest score you have ever obtained at cricket against the M.C.C. and Ground.'

In the following year a separate Criminal Investigation Department was formed, with a young barrister, Howard Vincent, at its head, with the title (adapted from the Paris police) 'Director of Criminal Investigations', and direct responsibility to the Home Office. (It was six years before the creation by Act of Parliament of a third Assistant Commissionership for the post rectified this anomaly.) Vincent's *Police Code* was the first attempt to set out the law and the policeman's duties under it, in simple language which could be easily understood by the average constable of those days. Running into many editions it was to remain a standard book for the police for more than half a century; but when it first came out, both *Punch* and *Moonshine* got hold of copies, and published extracts with satirical comments and illustrations.

As his right-hand man, he had Chief Superintendent Adolphus Williamson, an outstanding detective who was to be the first 'ranker' Chief Constable at Scotland Yard.* Bearded and always wearing a silk hat and a flower in his buttonhole, and nicknamed 'The Philosopher' by his colleagues, he was an easy subject for caricatures, sharing the

MOONSHINE'S INANIMATE OBJECTS

THE CLOCK TOWER—NOT CAPT. GOSSETT.   THE A DIVISION—NOT SERJT. DENNING.

[*Moonshine*, Feb. 17, 1883

honours with Inspector Ebenezer Denning, 'the Parliamentary Chief Bobby', with his goatee beard.†

* As a sergeant in the small detective branch nearly twenty years before, Adolphus Williamson had been assisting Inspector Whicher in the Constance Kent case. Whicher was the original of Sergeant Cuff in Wilkie Collins' novel *The Moonstone*; after retirement he was engaged to make private enquiries in the case of the Tichborne Claimant.

† Captain Gosset, who appears in the cartoon with Denning, was then on the verge of retiring from the post of Serjeant-at-Arms, after fifty years' service. (The Clock Tower, behind him, contains the prison rooms in which persons committed to his custody were detained.) Denning had been for twenty years so familiar and respected a figure, that *Vanity Fair* had a full-page cartoon of him by Pelegrini ('Ape'), with a biographical note:

'He attends every Sunday at St Margaret's Church to guard those seats reserved for Members of the House of Commons which no Member of the House was ever known to occupy. . . . He has been foremost in promoting the Police Orphanage at Twickenham. He is moreover a Sunday-school teacher, and has taken many prizes for fret-work.'

In 1878 Charles Peace was arrested after shooting at a constable at Blackheath, and ultimately executed for a murder in Sheffield two years before, confessing to many burglaries in the Blackheath area. *Punch* had now abandoned its earlier anti-capital punishment attitude, and defended the retention of the gallows; but they condemned the undue prominence given in the press to the personalities and tastes of criminals.

They continued to comment on the urbane inefficiency of the police force, especially what they had nicknamed 'The Defective Department' or 'The Criminal Instigation Department'. *Fun* published their own version of 'New Police Regulations for better regulation of the streets of the Metropolis after nightfall—"pending revival by the authorities of Scotland Yard of the curfew and the feudal system, with the police for the barons and the public for their vassals"'.

IN HOPES

Sergeant of Police (to Bobby). 'WHAT O'CLOCK IS IT?'
Bobby. 'I AIN'T GOT A WATCH.'
Sergeant. 'NOT GOT A WATCH! HOW LONG HAVE YOU BEEN IN THE FORCE?'
Bobby. 'THREE MONTHS, SIR.'
Sergeant. 'THREE MONTHS, AND NO WATCH!'
Bobby. 'PLEASE, SIR, I AIN'T HAD NO NIGHT DUTY YET.'

[*Judy*, Dec. 15, 1880

'All persons requiring the use of a latchkey will have to obtain a licence from
Scotland Yard to carry one. . . . Any unlicensed person found abroad with a latchkey
at any hour, to be hanged upon the nearest lamp-post. . . . All crowds or assemblages
of two or more persons in the streets after sunset will be treated as rioters.'

The year 1880 saw the production of the Gilbert and Sullivan opera *The Pirates of
Penzance*, with its chorus of policemen led by the sergeant who sings the immortal song
'A Policeman's Life is Not a Happy One', which was to be parodied many a time in
Punch.

I can find no reference in *Punch* to Paddington Pollaky, whose 'keen penetration'
was one of the attributes of W. S. Gilbert's Heavy Dragoon in *Patience*, produced at the
newly opened Savoy Theatre in 1881. He was a real-life detective, Ignatius Paul
Pollaky, attached to the Paddington Police Office.

About the same time the dialogue under a drawing in *Judy*, 'In Hopes', contains a
very uncomfortable innuendo. But tales of watches 'acquired' from persons found drunk
must have been supposed to have had a basis of truth over several decades, because the
suggestion appears in music-hall songs as far back as the 'sixties, and could still rouse
a guffaw in the 'nineties.* It even makes one wonder whether there must not have been
the same sly innuendo in the apparently innocent couplet

> 'Every member of the force
> Has a watch and chain of course'

in the well-known song 'If you want to know the time, ask a Policeman!' which James
Fawn first sang in the music-halls in 1889. (Maybe it was Mr Ingersoll who relieved

---

* One verse of 'Peter Potts the Peeler', which The Great Vance was singing in the 'sixties, ran:

> 'That all our men a watch can boast
> Is quite a matter of course, sirs!
> If they don't get one in a month at most
> We turn 'em out o' the Force, sirs!
> And often, too, in their first week,
> They finds a chap "in liquor",
> And it only wants a little cheek
> To be master of a "ticker".'

And late in the 'nineties, Herbert Campbell in his song 'The P.C.' was making the same point:

> 'I had one watch when I entered the p'lice,
>   Now I've got another one.
> One's no good to a guardian of the peace,
>   He must have two or three.
> If a great big toff should get a lot of wet,
> It's not my fault if he happens to forget
> That he had a five-guinea ticker when he met
>   This kind P.C.'

the pressure of temptation to 'help yourself' when he began shipping his famous five shilling watches across the Atlantic early in the 1900's.)

The footpad and the armed burglar were very much in the public mind about this time, and accompanying the full-page cartoon 'An Unequal Match', *Punch* had some verses which ended

'Bar his Colt, there's nought alarming
To a *man*, in Burglar Jim,
But if us you can't be arming,
'Ow about *dis*-arming him?'

AN UNEQUAL MATCH

[*Punch*, Oct. 8, 1881

A few months later *Punch* had another full-page cartoon entitled 'Murder Made Easy', in which a shop-keeper is shown saying to a tough criminal type:

'We only sell poisons to medical men; but anything in revolvers and dynamite.'

Shortly afterwards, when the police were having revolver drill, *Judy* printed some verses:

> 'Now Robert has a pistol,
> Just like William Sykes's hobby,
> So Bobby is a match for Bill,
> And ten to one on Bobby!'

It remained a perennial problem, whether police should carry firearms or not. In 1883 a solution was found by letting men on night duty in the outer areas carry stout sticks. In rural areas they were allowed to take their own dogs on patrol with them.

Punch had nothing but straightforward reporting about the opening of the new Law Courts in the Strand in 1882; but in the following year there was another full-page cartoon which showed Mr Punch telling a Director of the District Railway (recently completed to run underneath the new Victoria Embankment) that the smoke and fumes coming up through the air shafts from the underground trains was almost as great a nuisance as the roughs who frequented the Embankment at night—even though the first electric street lighting had recently been installed there.*

Any idea that the traffic problem at pivotal points in London is new, would be dispelled by a picture, 'Metropolitan Prize Puzzles No 1: Find the Policeman', which appeared in *Punch* in June 1883. It shows a solid jam of horse-drawn carriages, coaches and omnibuses, with top-hatted drivers and passengers, all trying to go different ways at Hyde Park Corner; the constable (if there at all) is quite invisible amongst them. Later there was another on similar lines, showing the hopeless state of traffic confusion in the Strand at the time the theatres 'broke'.

The 'New Police' had from the start taken over the functions of the old beadles or 'street keepers' in regulating traffic at important street junctions and keeping crossings clear for pedestrians, but had no specific legal powers to do so. Hyde Park Corner during 'the season' presented the biggest problem, in dealing with the assembly of private carriages. Long before the 'horseless carriage', traffic hold-ups for half an hour or an hour were—Arthur Bryant tells us—not uncommon. There were large numbers

---

* A popular song of the time, 'The New Electric Light', included the couplet:

> 'Policemen down the areas, then, must look out, or we might
> Find out where our pies and cold meat go to, by electric light.'

THE SPEED PEELER

'AMENITIES DENIED OUR FOREFATHERS'
[*Punch Summer Number*, 1936

of summonses for furious and reckless driving, ever since the Highway Act of 1835 had created these offences. Queen Victoria's coronation year had brought matters to a head, and under an Act of 1839 the Police of the Metropolis were for the first time recognised by statute as traffic controllers. The Great Exhibition of 1851 brought the first need for large-scale traffic control. Further police powers to make traffic regulations came in the 'sixties, when 'fixed points' were introduced.

The policeman's willingness—indeed his more than readiness—to come to the rescue of a lady in distress had been pictured in *Punch* at various times. Now there appeared some rather charming verses 'What will you do, ma'am?' of which one couplet will suffice:

> 'I stop the traffic at once for you.
> Take my arm, ma'am—I'll see you through!'

But Harcourt's defence of some slander was only half accepted. *Moonshine* had some verses recapitulating all the standard tales, under the title 'Have we done you wrong, Bobby?'

> 'Tales of viands cold, Bobby,
> In the area's gloom;
> Tales of stories told, Bobby,
> To the victim's doom.
> Tales of watch and chain, Bobby,
> *Found* at dead of night;
> Tales of persons slain, Bobby,
> Fits put down as "tight".
> Tales of belt and staff, Bobby,
> March of frog, severe;
> Glass of half-and-half, Bobby,
> No inspector near.'

WHEN DUTY IS A PLEASURE

Scene: Ludgate Circus.

Timid Little Person. 'POLICEMAN, THE ROAD IS SO CROWDED, DO YOU MIND SEEING ME ACROSS?'
Policeman (gallantly). 'MIND, MISS! SHOULDN'T I LIKE TO!'

[*Judy*, Oct. 29, 1879

THE IDOL OF THE DAY; OR, THE TRIUMPH OF BOBBY

[*Fun*, April 25, 1883

The police whistle gradually superseded the rattle in 1883—at first for day duty only. It had been tried in 1846, but they had gone back to the rattle. Now in *Punch* there were some verses 'The Whistling Bobby' and some criticism of what had apparently been the original proposal, that the whistle would be fixed on the end of the truncheon. *Punch* feared that this might lead to more frequent use of the truncheon. Misquoting parts of some new police regulations, *Punch* also suggested that, by the time a constable had made all the prescribed checks on a suspected housebreaker, the man would have left the scene, but the whistle would at any rate come in useful to start the pursuit.

A further series of dynamite outrages by Irish-American Fenians, including explosions in *The Times* office and in Scotland Yard itself, were to make the police the heroes of the hour. One explosion took place just outside the House of Commons in the middle of a speech, but no one in the chamber (we are told) turned a hair. It happened to be the day of the Oxford and Cambridge Boat Race, and next day Harcourt, the Home Secretary, came along in a hurry and demanded an instant increase of police numbers, explaining that the calls made on the police by the holding of the Boat Race had given desperadoes their opportunity. There was a rhyme in circulation for a time:

> 'Harcourty, Harcourty, hock—
> What caused the dynamite shock?
> The Blues and their races
> Drew Blues from their places—
> Harcourty, Harcourty, hock!'

A full-page cartoon in *Fun* shows 'Bobby, the Idol of the Day', being drawn on a triumphal chariot by Harcourt and Gladstone, then Prime Minister.

Sir William Harcourt has been summed up as a strong Home Secretary and a great fighter, who administered the criminal law with merciful fairness and gave much guidance to Scotland Yard, keeping in the foreground the importance of safeguarding the liberty of the individual.* There was a full-page cartoon of Mr Punch congratulating Harcourt on 'Our Dark Blue Line of Defence', quoting a speech in which he had said:

> 'Our first line of defence that we have is the police, and I hope I may pay my tribute to the splendid services which the Police, not only in the Metropolis, but also in the provinces, and above all in Ireland, have rendered to the cause of Society.'

* He was a grandson of the Archbishop of York, and a firm believer in capital punishment. (Later, as Chancellor of the Exchequer, he was to introduce death duties.) He also advocated the use of the birch instead of detention in prison for juvenile offenders. 'His recommendation', says a writer in the *Dictionary of National Biography*, 'led to a marked reduction in the number of juvenile criminal convictions.'

There were some laudatory verses in the same number, 'Punch to the Peelers':

> 'Civil servants in plain woollen stuff,
> Civic badge upon collar and cuff,
>   Yet cynics must own
>   Simple "Bobbies" have shown
> Something more of true soldiership tough
>   Than enough
> For mere dealing with burglar and rough.'

None the less, the comic papers never let up for long on their cartoons of Colonel Henderson as over-militarising the police.

ON THE TRACK
COLONEL HENDERSON AND THE MILITARY POLICE.

[*Fun*, Feb. 4, 1885

In the following year the 'Special Branch' of the **C.I.D.** was formed—originally as a 'Special Irish Branch'. Howard Vincent retired in that year (1884) to go into Parliament. In six years he had increased the strength of the C.I.D. from 250 to 800. But the popular idea that a plain-clothes man remained a policeman, and deceived no one, persisted. Both *Punch* and *Fun* had cynical drawings of 'The Undetectable Detective'.

DISGUISED—OR THE UNDETECTABLE DETECTIVE

[*Fun*, March 4, 1885

The post of Director of Public Prosecutions, created in 1879, was abolished in 1884, not to be re-created until 1908. *Punch* fairly frequently had adverse comments to make about the limited activities of the first holder of the office, including a full-page cartoon 'Now then, Mr Public Prosecutor, *wake up*!' and another of Mr George Lewis trying to 'wind him up'.

In 1884, the year of the Third Great Parliamentary Reform Bill, a cartoon in *Fun* showed Bobby thanking Gladstone in anticipation that he would at last get the vote.

'P'LICE, SIR!'

Mr Macliver. 'PERMIT ME TO INTRODUCE MY FRIEND, MR BOBBY, WHO, HEARING THAT YOU HAVE TAKEN UP THE FRANCHISE BILL, HOPES THAT YOU WILL RUN IN A VOTE FOR HIM.'
Mr Gladstone. 'I SEE NO REASON WHY YOU SHOULD NOT HAVE WHAT YOU ASK.'
Mr Bobby. 'THANK YOU, SIR; YOU MAY ALWAYS RELY ON US DOING OUR DUTY.'

[*Fun*, May 26, 1884

The policeman had been expressly excluded from the franchise ever since the founding of the force, lest there might be any suspicion of political partisanship in carrying out his duties. In fact it was another three years before a Police Disabilities Removal Act gave him the Parliamentary vote, and another six before he was to be allowed to vote at municipal elections.

Punch maintained its robust humanitarian attitude on the drink question, and sided with the moderate reformers. It recognised that the magisterial licensing system tended in practice to be vexatious, inconsistent and meddlesome; but teetotalism was to it inextricably associated with cranks, faddists and fanatics, while Sabbatarianism, it thought, drove men to drink. The inebriated 'swell' or the drunken cabby appeared frequently in its pages, and sometimes even the intoxicated constable, and were treated with tolerant humour.

It was coming to be generally recognised that police were being overburdened with 'extraneous duties', ranging from fire-brigade work to first aid; and *Fun* had a series of pictures, culminating in the suggestion that the 'omnificent' constable ought to be preserved under a glass case, instead of being exposed to all the risks of mad dogs and burglars' revolvers.

[*Fun*, July 1, 1885

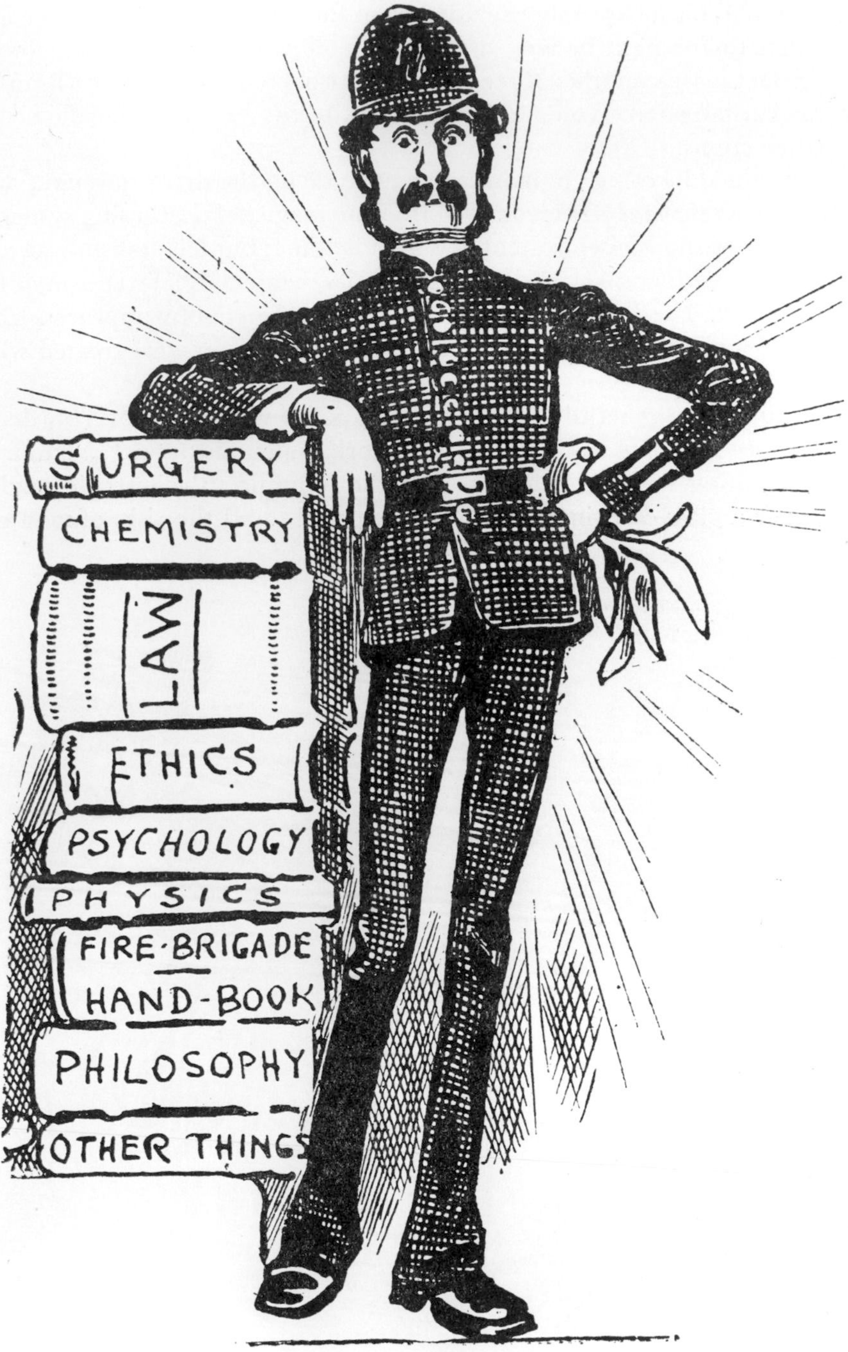
SURGERY
CHEMISTRY
LAW
ETHICS
PSYCHOLOGY
PHYSICS
FIRE-BRIGADE HAND-BOOK
PHILOSOPHY
OTHER THINGS

[*Fun*, July 8, 1885

It noted at the same time, however, that policemen seemed to thrive on their calling —as evidenced by the strip cartoon 'Increase of the police'.

'INCREASE' OF THE POLICE

FUN's readers have doubtless observed how splendidly members of 'the Force' thrive on their calling, their plumpness growing with their service. The Gentlemen in Blue depicted below will therefore easily be recognised as

A NOVICE   A TWO-YEARS' MAN   A FIVE-YEARS' MAN   A TEN-YEARS' MAN   A RETIRED VETERAN RECALLING THE
                                                                            DAYS OF HIS YOUTH

[*Fun*, July 1, 1885

Punch's 'Essence of Parliament' contained a brief reference to the passing of the Criminal Law Amendment Act of 1885. The Act was known as the W. T. Stead Act, after the then editor of the *Pall Mall Gazette,* who had been featuring a series of articles exposing the horrors of the white-slave traffic, under the title 'The Maiden Tribute of Modern Babylon'.* The Bill had been introduced primarily to make further provision for the protection of women and girls; but an additional clause rushed through by Labouchère at the third reading created a new offence which was to bear fruit in the Wolfenden Committee of recent times. There is no mention of this clause in Henry Lucy's 'Diary of Toby, M.P.', but his succinct summary of the proceedings is relevant.

> 'A quiet night. Very few here. Criminal Law Amendment Bill being discussed, with one eye on the Housing of the Working Classes Bill. If Criminal Law Amendment Bill were disposed of before half-past twelve, t'other would come on. But if talk can be kept up till 12.30, must stand over. So opponents of the Housing of Working Classes Bill talked at length on Criminal Law Amendment Bill up to half-past twelve. When clock struck half hour, talk suddenly collapsed. Criminal Law Amendment Bill passed.'

* W. T. Stead has been described by contemporary journalists as a hypocritical prude. The bitterness with which he thwarted every attempt by Sir Charles Dilke to re-enter public life after the notorious divorce case was particularly resented. At this time he had not yet founded his *Review of Reviews.* He was to live to go down in the *Titanic.*

Judy, inspired by a newspaper story that the wife of a provincial Chief Constable while up in London had recognised and been instrumental in the arrest of a wanted man, published another fanciful sketch of a policewoman, with the caption:

'We presume that on an early date we may find our muscular sisters joining the police force and becoming a terror to the gentle burglar.'

GOOD NEWS

[*Judy*, Aug. 5, 1885

Hard winters in those days meant skating everywhere; and this gave Charles Keene an opportunity for one more drawing of the ponderous policeman with the large beard,

DOUBTFUL

Ponderous Policemen (in chorus to Small Boys). 'HERE, YOU! MOVE OFF! THE HICE AIN'T SAFE!'

[*Punch*, Feb. 20, 1886

who appears in so many of his pictures. If the laugh is against the policeman it is a kindly one, and only another reminder of the policeman's instinctive selflessness in getting on with his duties of preserving the public safety.

8th February 1886 was known as 'Black Monday'. After rival meetings of the unemployed and the Social Democrats in Trafalgar Square, a small mob of roughs from the East End started a riotous procession through Pall Mall and St James's up to Oxford Street, throwing stones through the windows of clubs and shop-fronts. Police reserves were not available in time; and for the next few days there was something like a panic. *Fun* published a parody of the policemen's chorus from the *Pirates of Penzance*: 'Left in the cold to sing—Tarantara!' and *Punch* published 'The Song of Scotland Yard': 'Wait till the crowds roll by, Bobby!', a variation of the well-known ballad.

'THE GREAT UNEMPLOYED'

(THE CHIEF COMMISSIONER OF POLICE, FEB. 8, 1886, THE FIRST DAY OF THE RIOTING.)

[*Punch*, Feb. 20, 1886

Tenniel's cartoon in *Punch* of the Commissioner, 'The Great Unemployed', was unnecessarily cruel. Henderson was now sixty-five years old, but had in fact been out in plain clothes during most of the day in the Square—where the Chief Superintendent in charge had his own pockets picked in the crowd. As will be seen from the writing on one of the papers shown on his table, there had been another rabies scare, and *Punch* the week before had published a cynical version of the police orders as to the muzzling or unmuzzling of dogs, which, it was suggested, were superseded every few days by different ones.

Henderson resigned, after what amounted to public censure by a new Home Secretary. Hugh Erskine Childers had had a large hand in the abolition of transportation of convicts to the colonies, and had also while at the War Office been responsible for the abolition of flogging in the army. The day of the riots was his first day at the Home Office. It was generally felt that the Commissioner had not been given a free enough hand, but was now being made the scape-goat. *Moonshine* published an 'In Memoriam' verse: 'Toll for the suave', and *Judy* said:

> 'That you were not alone to blame
> Is what we all well know,
> But take your pension and depart,
> Ted Henderson my Jo.'

Judy also had some cynical verses headed 'The Cheerful Childers and the Bound Bobbies':

> 'He gave no orders to the Force
> To quell the furious riot;
> He said "Be neutral", which of course
> Meant "*You* alone be quiet."
>
> Bound hand and foot, each Bobby gazed
> Upon the Wreckers sadly,
> Who soon our West-End swells amazed
> By smashing windows madly.
>
> So charge your glasses to the brim,
> Ye glaziers and ye builders!
> Full many a pound you've made by him—
> This cheerful Mr Childers.'

Henderson was presented by the cab-proprietors and cab-drivers of London with a model in silver of the newest type of hansom cab, 'in acknowledgement and appreciation of his efforts to improve the social position of the London cabmen'; and there was much talk about who his successor would be. *Moonshine* published cartoons of the three most talked-of candidates—Lord Wolseley, the distinguished army reformer, on whom

W. S. Gilbert had modelled his 'Modern Major-General' in *The Pirates of Penzance*; Captain Shaw, the well-known and popular Chief of the Metropolitan Fire Brigade,*

THE CANDIDATES FOR THE CHIEF BOBBYSHIP

LORD WOLSELEY   CAPTAIN SHAW   MR HOWARD VINCENT

[*Moonshine*, March 13, 1886

and Howard Vincent, who was now in Parliament, having resigned from Scotland Yard two years before.

* In 1882 he had been sitting in the stalls at the Savoy on the opening night of *Iolanthe*, when the Fairy Queen sang:

> 'Oh, Captain Shaw,
> Type of true love kept under!
> Could thy brigade
> With cold cascade
> Quench my great love, I wonder!'

Again a soldier was appointed—General Sir Charles Warren, another R.E., recalled from a military command in Egypt. He had worked with Lord Wolseley, and had the reputation of a strong disciplinarian; but he had small knowledge of police affairs, and was deficient in tact. He had immense energy; but his imperious military attitude—'the iron hand without the velvet glove'—did not go down well with the police or the public. He was moreover in constant conflict with the Home Secretary and the permanent staff at the Home Office.

Childers—who was shortly to retire himself from ill-health—had lost no time in setting up a Committee to review the administration and organisation of the Metropolitan Police—a somewhat unusual committee, with himself as chairman, to report to himself. It was the opinion of that committee—and indeed the general opinion in the press—that the force, now 14,000 strong, needed more 'officers of superior rank and education or of experience in the habit of command', and they considered that 'retired Officers of the Army who shall have served with merit and occupy a certain social position' would be most suitable. Warren resuscitated the post of District Superintendent created by Henderson, giving it the title of Chief Constable. Of the original four posts two had been allowed to lapse, and the men filling the other two had gravitated to headquarters. Warren brought in five army officers; and *Punch* printed a cynical test paper to be answered by candidates for the post:

> 'Mention your rank in the Army, stating whether you have ever served as Field-Marshal or as General of a Division. . . . Mention if you can any of your ancestors who fell at the battle of Hastings, Agincourt, or in the Wars of the Roses. . . . Do you dine out frequently during the season? Give not less than fifteen addresses within a mile of Belgrave Square to which you have been invited. . . . Do you get asked anywhere into the country for the shooting, and do you show in the park in the season on a hired hack? Have you ever managed to get your name mentioned in the column of Fashionable Intelligence in the *Morning Post*? . . . Have you had any facilities of becoming acquainted with the working and ways of the police, other than of having been locked up in connection with a night-charge?'

Warren's short tenure of the post—he lasted two years and nine months—has been described as a signal instance of the failure of a military administration of the force; but pressure of events gave him little peace for the reorganisation which he conceived to have been the purpose of his appointment. Probably at no period have the police been so much in the public eye. In the years 1886–8 there were no fewer than sixteen full-page cartoons in *Punch*, and a dozen in *Fun*, as well as countless smaller satirical drawings about police in *Judy* and *Moonshine*.

Like both his predecessors, Warren quickly became involved in the vexed question of rabies and dog-muzzling orders. A well-known line of Virgil appeared in *Moonshine* as '*army wirumque cano*', loosely translated as 'The soldier shall muzzle the dog'. One police constable, bitten by a mad dog, was sent to Paris for treatment by M. Pasteur;

and *Moonshine* published a pair of cartoons of Warren and Pasteur, with their functions

SIR C. WARREN AS MONS.
PASTEUR

MONS. PASTEUR AS SIR C.
WARREN

[*Moonshine*, Oct. 9, 1886

transposed; while *Punch* had a picture of 'The policeman as he ought to be (properly protected)'.

THE DOG SCARE

THE POLICEMAN AS HE OUGHT TO BE (PROPERLY PROTECTED) OUTSIDE
THE SIX-MILE METROPOLITAN RADIUS.

[*Punch*, Nov. 6, 1886

There were labour troubles, too; but by November Mr Punch found it necessary to draw the Commissioner's attention good-humouredly to the need to deal with the prevalence of burglaries.

THE BURGLARIAN QUESTION

Mr Punch. 'BRAVO, SIR CHARLES! YOU'VE DONE CAPITALLY WITH THE DOGS AND DEMOCRATS. NOW, HOW ABOUT THE *BURGLARS*?'

Chief Commissioner of Police. 'ALL RIGHT, MR PUNCH! "MUCH HAS BEEN DONE, BUT MORE REMAINS TO DO"!'

[*Punch*, Nov. 20, 1886

Fictional detective stories were becoming popular by the 'eighties. Andrew Lang had some verses in *Punch* in 1885.

> 'Tell me not, O Soul that slumbers,
> "Life is placid, Life is pale."
> 'Tis not so in Christmas Numbers;
> *There* quite other views prevail.
>
> *Lives of Great Highwaymen* show it,
> How to make our lives sublime:
> Bother sense and grammar! Go it
> Give us something new in Crime!'

Conan Doyle took the tip, and Sherlock Holmes made his first appearance in 'A Study in Scarlet' in *Beeton's Christmas Annual* for 1887. He was by no means the first detective in English fiction. Edgar Allan Poe's *Dupin* stories had been published in the 'forties. Charles Dickens and Wilkie Collins had modelled Inspector Buckett and Sergeant Cuff on actual members of the original small detective branch at Scotland Yard. *Hawkshaw the Detective* and Tom Taylor's *Ticket-of-Leave Man* had been seen on the London stage in the 'sixties.

Queen Victoria's Jubilee naturally meant a great deal of police work in 1887, and *Punch* had a full-page cartoon, 'Punch to the Peelers' showing Mr Punch congratulating the Commissioner and the force:

> 'All honour to your management, my Warren,
>   All honour to the Force you featly led!
>
>   .   .   .   .   .
>
> Mr Punch from post of vantage proudly viewed them;
>   They combined unshrinking toil with ready tact,
> Whilst the sultry summer sunshine broiled and stewed them,
>   Showing judgment when to act or not to act.
> Their thin blue line kept order; firm yet kindly,
>   They stood with faces flushed, but pulses cool,
> Whilst the multitude around them crowded blindly,
>   True type of a free people's civic rule!'

But before July was out the Cass case was to bring the police into bad odour again. On Jubilee night a Miss Cass was arrested on a charge of soliciting in Regent Street. The conditions in Regent Street at night time had evidently been causing a good deal of concern, and the inability of the police to clean it up had led the Regent Street tradesmen to form a sort of vigilance committee of their own. *Punch* had a cartoon, with some verses ending 'Why should a man who keeps dogs have to bark?' Miss Cass managed to

LATEST STREET IMPROVEMENT

Regent Street Tradesman. 'LOOK HERE, MR POLICEMAN, AS WE WANT THE JOB OF CLEARING UP THIS PLACE WELL DONE, WE'LL DO IT OURSELVES.'

[*Punch*, July 16, 1887

convince the magistrate that she was a respectable lady taking a harmless walk; and was discharged. The Home Secretary mishandled the House in the debate which followed, and on a motion for adjournment the government were defeated. The constable concerned was suspended and charged with perjury, but enquiries meanwhile in her home town revealed that the lady was not so white as she had painted herself, and he was acquitted and honourably reinstated early in the following year. By then, however, mud had stuck, in the way it does; and *Punch* and *Fun* had cartoons of Warren whitewashing the police.

Matthews, the new Home Secretary, has been described as 'a departmental success
but a parliamentary failure'. Educated abroad, a catholic and a bachelor, he had been
called to the bar and appeared in both the Tichborne and the Dilke trials. He had only
had six years in Parliament, followed by a twelve-year gap; and now it was his personal
friendship with Lord Randolph Churchill, it is said, which led to his being given the
Home Office. Gladstone, Prime Minister for the third time, was largely preoccupied
with the Irish question. Labouchère in *Truth*, and W. T. Stead, then editor of the *Pall
Mall Gazette*, were always criticising Matthews's decisions. *Punch* gave him the title 'The
Not-At-All-At-Home-Secretary'; *Fun* called him 'The Home, Sweet Home Secretary'.

WAKING HIM UP
OR, THE SLEEPING BEAUTY OF THE HOME OFFICE
''TIS THE VOICE OF THE SLUGGARD—I HEARD HIM COMPLAIN.'

[*Fun*, Oct. 10, 1888

Constant friction between him and the combative and opinionated Warren was inevitable. During that summer, homeless unemployed took to camping in Trafalgar Square; charitably minded people distributed bread from vans; and the numbers were swollen by the roughs and scum of London, till thousands assembled there every night. Warren appears to have had little appreciation of much genuine hunger and distress, and was accused of a policy of military repression. There were questions in parliament and much comment in the press. Socialist agitators and demagogues took advantage of the distress, and preached violence. They also tried, with a meeting in Hyde Park joined by John Burns, to foment discontent in the force, where there was already some feeling about the system of promotion, as well as the long hours of duty. That summer and autumn the police were hard pressed and suffered much provocation, critics being always ready to accuse them of 'illegal and brutal conduct'. *Punch*, with a full-page cartoon, quoted Warren's statements in his published Annual Reports that the growth of London had outrun any increase in numbers of the force, and showed Police-Sergeant Punch interviewing 'would-be ex-unemployed' and suggesting that he might help enforce the law rather than break it.

The whole question of the right to hold public meetings in Trafalgar Square now became a political issue, from which in due course were to follow the present regulations, which allow meetings to be held there subject to prior notice to the Commissioner of Police. But in 1887 the matter hung on the Trafalgar Square Act of 1844, which had brought the area within the general provisions of the Metropolitan Police Acts. Inevitably the red herring of the Right of Free Speech was dragged across the issue, but this has nothing to do with it. There is no right in law to hold meetings on the highway or in public places.

Large numbers of police were being employed day after day in escorting processions through the streets of the West End. In the City processions were firmly dispersed; and there was some friction between the Commissioners of the two forces. Ultimately Warren issued an order forbidding processions to the Square to hold meetings there, which Matthews endorsed in a half-hearted way, but then began to wobble.

One of the first of F. Anstey's famous series '*Voces Populi*', which appeared in *Punch* on 29th October 1887, gives the impartial onlooker's point of view so well, that it is worth quoting fairly extensively.

'*SCENE—Trafalgar Square. Several thousand loafers and roughs discovered asserting right of free speech, free meeting and free procession. A few hundred genuine artisans out of work standing about moodily. Lines of policemen drawn up in reserve look on impassively.*'
Demagogue (*to Police Sergeant*). Now, don't you interfere—that's all *I* ask. *I'll* speak to them—I have them thoroughly in hand just now, but, if you offer them the least opposition, I—well, I won't be responsible for what happens. . . . Friends, you are met here in this peaceful but imposing manner in the teeth of a brutal and over-bearing Constabulary, to show the bloated capitalists that we mean to be taken seriously. . . .

(Throws open frock-coat, and displays thick gold watch-chain. . . . Mob pulls him down and attempts to take him to pieces.)

Demagogue. Here, hi, Policemen, help! Why the devil don't you use your staves? *(Is rescued and assisted home by Police.)*

A Rough *(to Policeman).* Keep moving? Ah, *I'll* move! *(Kicks him on the knee-cap. Policeman draws truncheon and hits back.)*

Crowd *(indignantly).* Boo! Coward! Strikin' a unarmed man—down with 'im! *(They beat brutal Constable to a jelly.)*

.   .   .   .   .

Professional *(emerging in opposite direction).* Three red clocks, two pusses, and a white slang; I ain't done so dusty! 'Ooray for the right o' Free Meetin', *I* sez!

Genuine Unemployed *(wearily).* Well, I dunno as I see what good all this 'ere is a goin' to do *hus*!

(And no more does Mr Punch.)'

From the start of the trouble *Punch* had been supporting Warren in the line he was taking, and suggested that the matter only needed to be referred to a Court of Common Sense. Now there was a full-page cartoon, reproving Matthews for interfering, and a short article starting 'Bravo, Sir Charles Warren!' and going on:

> 'The roughs may consider you a Rabid Warren, but your arrangements seem to be remarkably judicious. Mr Punch trusts that "the wandering bands perambulating the streets", which you are going to consider as disorderly, will be taken to include those disturbers of our Sunday Quiet, calling themselves Members of the Salvation Army. There are six days in the week for noise, and the Salvationists can let us have our Sunday in peace.'

It is strange to recall that that estimable organisation should have found itself, as it was in its early days, in need of police protection.

The question arose whether Warren's order would make the Lord Mayor's procession illegal; and there was another full-page cartoon showing Warren reassuring the Lord Mayor: 'You're not a "Procession"—you're a "Show". *You* won't "terrorise the inhabitants".'

In the same issue 'The Letter-Bag of Toby, M.P.' contained a long one 'from a Home Secretary', from which it is only possible to include extracts.

> 'I see by the papers that I am about to resign office,' he writes. 'It seems odd that the office should be so much hankered after by men of various temperaments. My old friend and patron Randolph fancies it would suit him down to the ground. I would like to see him at the Home Office, if only for a short six months. The post, of course, has its attractions. But to tell the truth, dear Toby, the Home Secretary is too close to, and frequently under, the public eye. He is, necessarily, always at

THE NOT-AT-ALL-AT-HOME SECRETARY

Mr General-Inspector Punch. 'NOW THEN, MATT, MOVE ON! DON'T INTERFERE WITH THE POLICE IN THE EXECUTION OF THEIR DUTY.'

('*The change of tactics last week on the part of the Police, in permitting a Meeting in Trafalgar Square, was said to be due to the interference of the Home Secretary.*'—*Daily Papers.*)

[*Punch*, Nov. 5, 1887

home to impertinent lookers-in, or idle callers who have not sufficient business of their own to attend to. If anything goes wrong with the water or the gas, if a country Magistrate makes a more than usually particular ass of himself, if a policeman arrests the wrong woman in Regent Street, if there is a procession through the parks or a meeting in Trafalgar Square, it's ever the Home Secretary that is wrathfully turned to for explanations. When things go well with London or the Provinces, you never hear the Home Secretary's name mentioned. On the other hand, if the least thing connected with his department goes wrong, he is held personally responsible, and the fiendish newspapers fall upon him.'

The letter, which purported to be signed 'H-nry M-tth-ws', and to be written from 'the sweet seclusion of Surrey', appeared in the issue dated Saturday, 12th November. It also includes the prophetic plaint:

'I used once to have Sunday to myself; but now, owing to the new-born church-going fervour of the Unemployed, Sunday is the worst day of the week.'

''TWAS IN TRAFALGAR SQUARE'

Nelson. 'AVAST THERE! SHIVER MY COLUMN! BRITON AGAINST BRITON?—A LANDLUBBER WAR IN MY SQUARE—THIS IS NOT WHAT "ENGLAND EXPECTS"!'

Warren. 'WAR?—MY DEAR HORATIO! NOT AT ALL. WE ARE MERELY DISCUSSING THE RIGHT OF PUBLIC MEETING!'

[*Fun*, Nov. 23, 1887

Henderson had met his Waterloo on 'Black Monday'. Sunday, 13th November became known as 'Bloody Sunday'. It was a trial of strength between the police and agitators. A number of processions converged from all directions on the Square, from which ordinary vehicular traffic had not been diverted. The result was confusion. The police had hoped to disperse the processions before they got there; but they were taken by surprise by some. Demonstrators carried iron bars and knives; and the crowd attempted to re-capture flags and banners taken from them by the police. There were baton charges by mounted police down Whitehall. Two squadrons of the Life Guards stationed in reserve had to be called out, a magistrate riding with them to read the riot act. Seven thousand special constables were also on duty. *Fun* published a cartoon showing Nelson coming down from his column to protest.

The year 1888 was the year of the Local Government Act, under which the London County Council was born, and in its early days aspired unsuccessfully to obtain control of both the Metropolitan and the City of London police forces—as town councils outside London had always had over borough police forces. Fifty of the smaller boroughs were however now to see their separate police forces merged in the county constabularies, for which the local J.P.s now had to share responsibility with the new county councils.

Unemployed demonstrations went on; but the most memorable event of the year was the 'Jack the Ripper' scare. The name originated from the signature of a letter in

red ink, sent to the Central News Agency and passed by them to Scotland Yard—
probably a hoax, but treated perhaps too seriously. The story is familiar from many
books. Certainly five murders of street women in Whitechapel, with atrocious mutila-
tions, between the 31st August and the 9th November 1888 are attributed to the sex

WHITECHAPEL, 1888

First Member of 'Criminal Class.' 'Fine body o' men, the per-leece!'
Second Ditto. 'Uncommon fine!—It's lucky for hus as there's sech a bloomin' few on 'em!!!'

[*Punch,* Oct. 13, 1888

maniac who was never identified. The crimes spotlighted the appalling conditions of poverty and vice in the East End. Tenniel had three grim cartoons in *Punch*—'Blind-Man's Buff (as played by the Police)', which showed the constable, with his eyes bandaged, surrounded by four laughing criminal types; and 'The Nemesis of Neglect' with some rather turgid verses, too long to quote in full:

> '. . . Ask purblind Municipal Muddledom
> The true significance of the City slum.
>   . . . Lurking crime
> Haunts from of old these dens of darksome slime.
> There, where well-armed Authority fears to tread,
> Murder and outrage rear audacious head.
> . . . This obscene Alsatia of the Slums.
> Town's carrier-hordes flock hither; hither comes
> The haggart harpy of the pavement, she
> The victim's victim, whose delirious glee
> Makes mirth a crackling horror; hither slink
> The waifs of passion and the wrecks of drink.
> No light there breaks upon the bludgeoned wife,
> No flash of day arrests the lifted knife,
> There shrieks arouse not, nor do groans affright.
> These are but normal noises of the night
> In this obscure Gehenna. . . .
>   . . . At Law the ghoul may laugh,
> The sword is here as harmless as the staff
> Of crippled age; its sleuthhounds are at fault,
> Justice appears not only blind but halt.
> It seems to play a merely blinkered game,
> Blundering about without a settled aim.'

So great was the panic in Spitalfields, Whitechapel and Stepney that Vigilance Committees were formed by the tradesmen, and the local M.P. offered a reward, to be followed by others. The press and politicians were attacking the alleged incompetence and bad leadership of the police; and even Queen Victoria wrote from Windsor: 'The Queen fears that the detective department is not so efficient as it might be.' As one murder succeeded another, there were constant questions in the House of Commons. Matthews was perpetually interfering and complaining to Warren, telling him and the Assistant Commissioner of the C.I.D. from time to time that he held them responsible for quicker results. Warren in turn was complaining that he was not given enough discretion. He wanted to issue notices offering rewards for information, but these were frowned on by the Home Office, where the view that this did more harm than good had held the field since Harcourt had enunciated it. He also made some rather ludicrous experiments with bloodhounds, against the advice of all his experts: *Punch* had an amusing account of the trials held in Hyde Park.

ANOTHER MISS

Keeper Matthews. 'P'RAPS IF YOU WAS TO SHOOT A LITTLE STRAIGHTER, SIR——'
Sir Charles. 'DON'T TALK TO ME; IT'S THE WIND, AND THE GUN'S WRONG, AND IT'S ALL YOUR FAULT—YOU'RE ALWAYS GETTING IN THE WAY.'

[*Fun*, Oct. 3, 1888

The murders all occurred on the borders of the Metropolitan Police District and the City, and there was some friction between the respective Commissioners. Though Warren had not much understanding or sympathy with the C.I.D., and tended to assess problems in military terms, everyone was on their toes, and there were many false arrests and false alarms. R. L. Stevenson's *Dr Jekyll and Mr Hyde* had appeared only a year or two before, and just now there was a play about it on in London; and this doubt-less put alarming ideas into people's heads.

Punch continued to support Warren.

'Those who join in blood-hounding him down must be interested in renewing the scenes of riot and disorder in Trafalgar Square with which Sir Charles dealt most effectively', a paragraph ran. 'The Police Force requires strengthening, and Sir Charles is perfectly alive to the fact.'

They had not been able to refrain, in a series of extracts from 'A Detective's Diary', from poking fun at the inefficiency of the C.I.D.; but they were also criticising the amateur crime investigators in stage plays, besides pointing out from time to time how much the police were hampered in their work by articles in the 'gutter press', giving the personal stories of criminals, and publicity to the movements of detectives, whose footsteps were dogged by reporters. In a burlesque comic opera scene—it would be almost as apposite today—in which 'A Dismayed Detective' is shown hotly pursued by a crowd of sensation-mongers, criminals and sub-editors, all demanding more details of what he is doing, the Chief Commissioner enters and sings:

'When tracking some terrible crime,
    For a moment the force seems at fault,
And Justice appears for a time
    To be baffled, and beaten, and halt.
When no clue on the surface is seen,
    And the trail is obscure and effaced,
Do you think the Detective's so green
    As to let you know all he has traced?
Surely, goodness alone knows what next you'll expect!
You forget a Detective is meant to *detect*.

So it isn't by showing his hand,
    Or supplying the needs of the Press
With a sketch of the scene he has plann'd,
    That his efforts he'll crown with success;
But by keeping the threads that he's got
    To himself, careful no chance to miss.
        Well, he tracked out the dynamite plot—
    Ten to one he'll make something of this!
But that you'll share his confidence, pray don't expect,
Bear in mind a Detective is meant to *detect*!'

The press generally were being frank in their criticisms of the whole regime. There were some verses in *Fun*:

'The spirit of Scotland Yard
May seem to live and grow;
But is it the best
In which one could invest?
   That's what we want to know.'

Warren's final effort had been to order a photographer to take a close-up picture of the dead woman's eyes—which finally disproved the popular superstition that a portrait of the last person seen was recorded there.*

He was to resign in November, after having written without permission a highly controversial article which was published in *Murray's Magazine*, dealing with the management of the police. He had fought all the time against interference and red-tape 'civilian control' from the Home Office, and resented any interference by the permanent staff, defending the force against unjust strictures. He took the stand that his own functions were clearly defined by statute, and the Secretary of State could not issue orders to the force nor apply the Official Secrets Act to him.

Punch had some verses:

'Who chased Cock Warren?
"I," said the Home Sparrow,
"With my views cramped and narrow,
I chased Cock Warren!"

And who'll fill his place?
"Why, I," said Monro.
"I'm the right man, I know,
And I'll fill his place."

And who'll tie your hands?
"Oh, I!" said Routine,
"That my business has been;
So I'll tie his hands." '

Fun had a cartoon suggesting that Matthews ought to 'Follow My Leader'; and in the music-halls Harry Randall was bringing the house down nightly with another parody of the nursery rhyme:

* The same superstition was to crop up forty years later, when P.C. Gutteridge had been shot in the eyes by Browne and Kennedy in Essex.

'FOLLOW MY LEADER'

A Suggestion, respectfully Dedicated to the Right Hon. Henry Matthews, M.P., Q.C., Home,
Sweet Home Secretary.

[*Fun*, Nov. 21, 1888

'Who killed Cock Warren?
"I," said the Home Sec.,
"I broke his neck;
I killed Cock Warren."

Who'll toll the bell?
"Matthews," said all,
"For he's next to fall;
He'll toll the bell."
And the roughs in the Square fell a-sighin' and a-sobbin'
When they heard of the death of poor Cock Warren.'

General Warren went back to the army, saw active service in the South African
War, and was helping Baden Powell to launch the Boy Scout movement in 1908.

On the question of a successor, after two resignations following so closely on each
other, *Punch* published some verses with their cartoon 'Extremes Meet':

EXTREMES MEET

Sir Edmund. 'MY DEAR WARREN, YOU DID TOO MUCH!'
Sir Charles. 'AND YOU, MY DEAR HENDERSON, DID TOO LITTLE!!'
Mr Punch (sotto voce). 'H'M!—SORRY FOR THE *new man*??'

[*Punch*, Nov. 24, 1888

' "Force is no remedy". This doctrine mad
Was held by some of Liberty's loud zealots.
"How, save by force, is Order to be had
'Midst a mixed horde of millionaires and helots?"

One Chief was sacked because he let the clutch
Of Anarchy come close, and did too little.
Another one because he did too much,
(Or, so some said: "Nay, not a jot or tittle!")

Power may at the implication chafe;
Police may fume at the implied comparison;
But *is* the Citadel entirely safe
Whilst there is angry strife amidst the garrison?'

As 'the New Man' who had Mr Punch's sympathy, James Monro was brought back. After police experience in Bengal, where he had been Inspector-General of Police, he had succeeded Howard Vincent as head of the C.I.D., but had found it impossible to work with Warren, and had resigned only four months before. He too was to have his troubles with Matthews and the Home Office, being opinionated also, though in a different way from Warren.

There were still difficulties with unemployed demonstrations, and renewed threats of Fenian outrages; and on top of it all he found himself, like his predecessors, involved in the unpopular enforcement of dog-muzzling orders.

OUR POPULAR SONGS ILLUSTRATED

No. 1 'The Lost Chord'

[*Fun*, Dec. 5, 1888

There was another East End murder of the Jack the Ripper type—though probably only imitative—in the summer of 1889. Monro was asking for a substantial increase in numbers—for which he had to wait another year—and the Annual Report, in which he had stated that the demands made on the resources of the force left them unable to give the police protection which the public expected, produced the cartoon 'Argumentum ad Pocketum' in *Punch*. Although the overall cost of police was then less than

'ARGUMENTUM AD POCKETUM'

Mr Bull (reads Yearly Police Report). 'WHAT'S THIS! INCREASE OF CRIME—NOT ENOUGH POLICE FOR THE PROTECTION OF LIFE AND PROPERTY! THEN, WHY ON EARTH—'
Chief Commissioner. 'YOU CAN HAVE ANY NUMBER OF POLICE, MR BULL—*IF YOU LIKE TO PAY FOR THEM!*'

[*Punch*, July 27, 1889

one-tenth of what it is today, the Exchequer grant was still limited to half the cost of pay and clothing; and the local authorities, who had to meet not only the other half but the full cost of everything else, including housing and pensions, stone-walled anything which would increase the police rate. But some not very distinguished verses in *Punch* through the mouth of 'Policeman X' bear witness to the state of friction between the Commissioner and the Home Office, and its effect on the force.

> '*I* don't care much who bosses us, so as the bossing is done clever,
> And ain't all shift and shindying. This style, though, can't go on for ever.
> Can't *someone* settle the whole thing upon a basis sound and stable,
> And not keep up this bad old game of Pot and Kettle, Cain and Abel?
> If I lets a street-spouter rave, Property drops on me a smasher,
> Whilst if I land him on the nob, Poverty calls me "brutal basher".
> If a Beak backs me from the Bench, scribes bully me in every journal,
> And, if the papers praise me, I may get the sack. The game's infernal!
> *I* do not want to brain stray curs, or *baton* Socialists or Paddies.
> That's a wild fancy of the raving Reds, fierce Rads, and frothing faddies,
> At present it's a Will-o'-the-Wisp, and I am weary of pursuing it,
> Jest tell me what my bizness *is*, my lords, and—*back me up in doing it* !'

In the autumn of that year came the great Dock Strike. With unobtrusive arrangements, Monro dealt well with the inevitable disturbances and the complaints which followed; but he found Matthews unhelpful and vacillating. Violent crime meanwhile continued; and *Punch* was continually advocating the 'cat' for armed burglars, and had a full-page cartoon of Bill Sykes, the injured innocent, complaining 'Do they want to make a brute o' me?'

Punch was also asking 'Is there, or is there not, a Public Prosecutor?' The functions were now merged in those of the Treasury Solicitor; but *Punch* was saying that, though absent from the courts, he was probably never absent on quarter-day, since Whitaker still showed £3,000 per annum as the salary of a 'Solicitor and Public Prosecutor'.

Matthews was having no easy time, with a series of difficult murder cases on which he had to decide whether to yield to strong representations and recommend reprieves. One case was that of Mrs. Maybrick, who some people were convinced had been wrongly convicted of poisoning her husband with arsenic from fly-papers. Another was a murderer named Lipski: there was a storm of protest at Matthews's decision not to recommend a reprieve, and it was only a confession on the eve of execution that saved Matthews once more from being driven from office. In *Punch* there was another cartoon of a harassed Home Secretary being comforted by Mr Punch with the suggestion that a Court of Criminal Appeal should be set up—but the country had to wait nearly twenty years longer for that.

THE ONLY REMEDY

Home Sec. 'OH, DEAR! OH, DEAR! WHY LEAVE IT TO ME!'

Mr Punch (*sympathetically*). 'WHY INDEED. BUT I DON'T SEE ANY HELP FOR IT TILL WE GET A COURT OF CRIMINAL APPEAL.'

[*Punch*, April 19, 1890

Monro resigned in June 1890, after being Commissioner for only eighteen months, and devoted the rest of his life to founding and carrying on a medical mission in Bengal. An impatient idealist, he had enlisted the press against the Home Secretary, and quixotically sacrificed his career rather than have a part in what he considered inadequate concessions to the men's claims to improvements in pay and pension with which he sympathised. The Police Act of 1890 was to make liberal provision as to pensions, and gave to police of all forces for the first time a statutory right to retire on half-pay after twenty-five years' service with a pension for life, increased to two-thirds after they completed twenty-six. It was to remain the policeman's charter for the next thirty years. An increase of pay also followed. But Monro had been continually urging the Home Office to be quicker about it, and did not wait to see how far the ultimate decisions would alleviate the smouldering discontent in the force. His resignation was deeply regretted in the force, where there was a general feeling that he had been pushed out. *Punch* had a full-page cartoon of Matthews 'the Not-quite-at-Home Secretary' singing 'in his Unpopular Entertainment':

'Why *did* Monro resign?
Was it any fault of mine?
If you want to know the truth—
          Ask the p'liceman!'

while *Fun* published a cartoon by Carruthers Gould of the Commissioner and the Home Secretary as Codlin and Short of Dickens's *Old Curiosity Shop*.

BOBBY'S DILEMMA

'REMEMBER, MY DEAR, CODLIN IS THE   'REMEMBER, MY DEAR, SHORT IS THE
FRIEND—NOT SHORT.'   FRIEND—NOT CODLIN.'—*Old Curiosity Shop*.

[*Fun*, June 25, 1890

So ended what is probably the most troublous period in the history of the Metropolitan Police, in which the press were more outspoken about Home Secretaries and Commissioners than at any time before or since. The last four years had seen three changes of Commissioner. The two who followed them were to hold the post for thirteen and fifteen years respectively, and were each to see half a dozen Home Secretaries in and out.

CHAPTER IV

Anarchists, Finger-prints and the Horseless Carriage

ALMOST immediately after taking office the new Commissioner found himself involved in the move of the headquarters down Whitehall to New Scotland Yard.

LAW v. MUSIC

The site once intended for the New Opera House, on the Victoria Embankment, is to be utilised for the Central Metropolitan Police Offices—*Daily Paper*.

Policeman X. 'WHAT ARE YOU A-DOING A-LOITERING 'ERE! THE PUBLIC DON'T WANT YER, AND I WANT THIS 'ERE GROUND MYSELF! SO COME, MOVE ON!'

[*Punch*, Aug. 14, 1886

The original offices in 4 Whitehall Place, backing onto Great Scotland Yard, had long become too small; but in the few years' interval since plans had been drawn up by Norman Shaw, the new building was already not big enough; so that the Lost Property Office and the Public Carriage Office had to stay behind for a year or two, until separate offices were made for the Receiver and his staff. *Punch* let the actual move pass unnoticed; but a cartoon '*Law* v. *Music*', which had appeared when it was first decided upon in

1886, recorded the past history of the site on the new Victoria Embankment. Much had already been done to reclaim this boggy patch of land between Cannon Row and Richmond Terrace for a Grand National Opera House, which was to have been erected there. That building, begun in 1875, had been nearly completed, but had failed for want of funds, and had ultimately been pulled down. The original foundations remained; the still existing subterranean passages had been intended to make it easy for patrons from the Houses of Parliament and the District Railway to reach the opera house.

Colonel Sir Edward Bradford, who was appointed to succeed Monro, had had a distinguished career in the Indian Army, but he had been chosen for his administrative rather than his military experience, having for several years been holding political appointments in India and at the India Office. He knew how to combine firmness in handling men with tact and diplomacy in his dealings with the Home Office; and *Punch* could not find grounds for suggesting that the police were being militarised, as the cartoons frequently published of Henderson and Warren had done.

Bradford had not been Commissioner for long before he became involved like his predecessors in the unpopular dog-muzzling regulations. A picture in *Punch* illustrated the sort of problems the poor policeman was up against. It was not until 1899 that *Punch* could print a full-page cartoon showing dog owners finally emancipated from the obligation to muzzle them.

THE MUZZLING REGULATIONS
ANOTHER CULPRIT

[*Punch*, March 14, 1896

Fingerprints had already been in use in India for a number of years, and interest in the subject was spreading; but ten years more were to elapse before they were officially adopted at Scotland Yard. Meanwhile the first joking reference to them appeared in *Judy* in 1891—two years before Asquith as Home Secretary was to set up a committee to enquire into their possibilities as a means of identification of criminals. Quoting a report of a discussion at a meeting of the Royal Society, *Judy* published a picture with some facetious verses:

[*Judy*, July 1, 1891

'No more the prints of hobnailed boots the bobby cute shall gauge
When forth he starts a crime to track, a criminal to cage.
No matter now how thick and deep the damning footprints fall,
He'll search for dirty finger-marks upon the tell-tale wall.
And, having found and studied these, his intellect acute
Will grasp at once who made the mark beyond the least dispute.
Once having settled this, he'll start upon the cheerful plan
Of taking everybody up—except the proper man.
So tracing crime by finger-marks may very likely come
To much resemble after all the good old rule of thumb.'

Things were on the whole easier for the police in the 'nineties, and *Punch*—with an easy-going editor—had less to say about their affairs. Both the police and the public needed to recuperate; and the thirteen years of Bradford's Commissionership were a relatively quiet period, and relations between police and public improved. But he had inherited a legacy of discontent, and a police strike broke out within a month of his taking up office. The Social Democratic Union had for some time been endeavouring at Hyde Park meetings to foment genuine police grievances about pay, pensions, hours of duty, promotion and punishments. Although the new police Bill already in print showed generous pension terms, its publication did not quench the smouldering discontent. The formation of a police union and the holding of meetings had been banned, and disciplinary action against the secretary of the men's committee ignited the fuse. On a Saturday evening in July 1890 more than a hundred men at Bow Street refused duty. They were immediately suspended, and the attempts to precipitate a general police strike failed; but very large crowds of outsiders—both agitators and roughs ready to join in any trouble—gathered in Bow Street that night, and mounted constables had to be reinforced by Life Guards from Knightsbridge Barracks. Rain helped.

'All the Police having now been replaced by Amateur Special Constables, who are as yet unfamiliar with their duties,' said *Punch*, in one of its few brief references, and went on to forecast the spread of the strike fever through the Metropolitan Magistrates, the High Court, the Church and the Medical Profession to the House of Commons. In another paragraph there was a rather feeble pun, describing as 'The Washerwoman's Clause' one of the men's demands:

'Duty to consist of eight hours *in one shift* out of every twentyfour.'

In his 'Essence of Parliament', Toby M.P. summarised proceedings in the House on the Metropolitan Police Vote:

'Home Secretary in the Dock; Sir William Harcourt, Q.C. prosecuted. Prisoner conducted his own defence. After long consultation, Jury could not agree, and were discharged without a verdict.'

A fortnight later, however, the Commons passed the second reading of the Police Bill without a division. Matthews was still Home Secretary and once more weathered the storm, but was to depart two years later on change of government.

Perhaps as an aftermath of the strike, perhaps because of some current case in the courts, now forgotten, the periodical idea again became general gossip, that police evidence is inspired more by comradely loyalty than by a strict regard for the truth.

In September 1891 a cynical cartoon 'Nothing but the Truth' by Tenniel appeared in *Punch*. The caption is self-explanatory.

NOTHING BUT THE TRUTH

Inspector. 'NOW SWEAR! ALL TOGETHER!'   *Constables.* 'WE SWEAR!!'
Mr Punch (*aside*). 'DEAR ME, SIR EDWARD; WHEN THEY *DO* AGREE, THEIR UNANIMITY IS
WONDERFUL!'—'*The Critic*,' *freely adapted.*

[*Punch*, Sept. 12, 1891

At this time a person charged with a criminal offence still could not go into the witness-box for his own defence (nor could the wife or husband). Lord Halsbury, the Lord Chancellor, was advocating in 1891 that the law should be changed; and *Punch*, under a full-page cartoon by Linley Sambourne of Halsbury inviting Bill Sykes to step into the witness-box, printed a parody of the Lord Chancellor's Song from *Iolanthe*:

'The law *should* be the embodiment
Of everything that is excellent.
But I fancy I've found one diminutive flaw
In that else impeccable thing, the Law.

As its constitutional guardian, I
Must extract that mote from the legal eye.
It seems a preposterous paradox
To exclude the accused from the Witness Box.

To alter that is a duty for
A very unprejudiced Chancellor.

If you step inside—as I trust you will—
We shall worm out the truth with forensic skill;
And if you decline—as I hope you won't—
We shall know there are reasons, friend, why you don't.

The triumph of Truth is a triumph for
A highly inquisitive Chancellor!'

(The Act, which was not passed for another seven years, contains safeguards for the prisoner on these and other points.)

The year 1892 is memorable for two things: Gladstone began his fourth and last premiership; and the name 'influenza' was invented for a mysterious new epidemic, which carried off a great many people, including the Duke of Clarence.

Anarchists—mainly Italian and Spanish refugees—were giving the police a good deal of trouble, during the next four years, with their constant threats of dynamite

RECKONING WITHOUT THEIR HOST

First Anarchist. 'ENFIN, MON AMI!—VE SHALL NOT BE INTERRUPT IN ZIS FREE ENGLAND!'

Bull A 1 (*sotto voce*). 'DON'T BE TOO SURE, MOSSOO! YOU'LL FIND NO *EXTENUA-TING CIRCUMSTANCES* HERE!!'

[*Punch,* May 7, 1892

outrages.* *Punch* had several full-page cartoons by Tenniel, with accompanying verses. In the first, P.C. Bull is warning refugees:

> 'Our Isle's immunity you boast!
> You're reckoning without your host.'

France was having similar problems, but apparently stumbling over the definition 'political offence', and criticising Great Britain for sentencing known anarchists to imprisonment. In another cartoon P.C. Bull is shown saying to a Sergent-de-Ville:

> 'You've my warmest sympathy,
> Victim of the new Red Terror.
>
> Amnesty to Anarchy
> Means encouragement to Murder!'

In a full-page cartoon by Linley Sambourne, 'Alien Anarchist' was shown, apologising to the Home Secretary: 'My comrades forgot; we are permitted to plot here, but our murders should be done abroad.' (But that was after the Tottenham affray, fifteen years later, when Russian and Polish refugees had become the main trouble-makers.)

Before the epidemic of the early 'nineties was over, the French President was to be assassinated by an Italian anarchist. By then 'The Allied Anarchist Groups of London' had even applied for police permission to hold a meeting in Trafalgar Square: the application was only refused after being carefully considered by the highest authority! Mr Punch reminded the Home Secretary of the troubles of 1887 and advised him: 'Prevent, don't wait to cure!' Another cartoon shows an anarchist who has gone too far and set British workmen booing, appealing to the police for help; the Constable replies: 'Down with everything, indeed! Lucky for *you* you haven't "downed" *me*!'

In 1893 Eros, the memorial to the Earl of Shaftesbury in Piccadilly Circus, was at last unveiled. *Punch* had been complaining for some time about the scaffolding which had been up since 1886. It was many years later when a cartoon by E. H. Shepard portrayed 'Mr Punch's simple suggestion for preventing any maltreatment of the figure'.

1893 was the year in which Paderewski's appearances in London caused such uncontrollable demonstrations by women admirers that *Punch* suggested police protection

---

* One of them, named Bourdin, on his way to blow up Greenwich Observatory, blew himself to pieces with his own bomb. Joseph Conrad based the character of Verloc on him in his story *The Secret Agent*, published in 1907, when the Assistant Commissioner, who figures a lot in the book, was modelled on Sir Melville Macnaghten.

AREN'T THEIR STATUES WONDERFUL?

(Mr Punch's simple suggestion for preventing any maltreatment of the figure of
Eros in Piccadilly Circus)

[*Punch*, March 31, 1937

on the concert platform. (E.T. Reed, the cartoonist, had a way of vulgarising any face; and he was fond of putting a policeman of similar type in the background in a great many of the parliamentary sketches which he was to do regularly in the years following.)

POLICE PROTECTION FOR PIANISTS!!

Made necessary by the antics of the Padded-roomski Devotees at St. James's Hall, who rush at, try to embrace, and deck with Roses, a certain Master whenever he appears.

[*Punch*, Nov. 11, 1893

The first electric street lighting installed in the City inspired *Punch* to some verses in which Bill Sikes complains:

'The Lights o' London? Yah! That's bin all boko.
Were London *lighted*, how could you and me
Garrotte a swell, or give a tight 'un toko?
We ain't got arf a chance where coves can *see*.'

Punch had always been strongly in favour of the use of the 'cat' on violent criminals, and had more than one cartoon showing Bill Sikes protesting that he would not like it. Now there was a parody of the Police Sergeant's song from *The Pirates of Penzance*, of which a few stanzas may be quoted:

'When the Cat was laid about the brute garrotter—cur garrotter,
He soon found it inadvisable to choke—'ble to choke.
The "corner-boys" and larrikins and such-like—louts and such-like—
Who rove the streets at night in rowdy gangs—robber gangs—
The tingling o' the nine tails might not much like—*would* not much like—
But *that* need not stir sentimental pangs—maudlin pangs.
Ah, take one consideration with another—with another,
The "Cat" should wake again, says *Punch* for one—*Punch* for one.'

A heat-wave in the summer of 1893 prompted more than one drawing and paragraph suggesting that the constable should have a lighter tunic for summer wear; but it was another four years before this was put into effect.

The year 1892 saw the first appearance in *Punch* of Phil May's drawings. He had already made his name in other journals; and his wonderful understanding of the life of the streets, where the police are involved, is illustrated by 'What's 'e done, Governor?'*

'WHAT'S 'E DONE, GOVERNOR?'

[*Punch, Annual,* 1892

* Phil May did a parody of this drawing himself, with a portrait of his publisher, and a variation in the caption: '*Who's* 'e done, Governor?' (In this he was following Lord Byron, whose 'Barabbas' bible, privately printed, had only one variation from the Authorised version: '*Barabbas was a publisher.*')

Before he was twenty, when he was employed as a stage decorator, he had been commissioned to decorate the Chief Constable's room in the Town Hall at Leeds.

By 1903 Phil May was dead—still under forty—having burnt out his candle by hard drinking.

Although the 'Horseless carriage' had begun to make its appearance on the roads quite early in the 'nineties, it was some years before it is mentioned in *Punch* at all. The standing traffic problem was 'the Society Crush at Hyde Park Corner' in 'the Season'. Now the bicycling craze made new problems; and a parody of the song 'Daisy Bell' (which Katie Lawrence first sang in the music-halls in 1892) appeared in *Punch* in 1893, under the title 'The Bicycling Cad'.

> 'Blazy, Blazy, Give me a chance, Sir, do!
> I'm half crazy All for the fear of you.
> You haven't a stylish way, Sir,
> I can't admire that blazer,
> (Which you think sweet.)
> The curse of the street
> Is the Bicycling Cad—like you!'

SUNDAY MORNING

Cyclist (to rural policeman). 'NICE CROWD OUT THIS MORNING!'
Rural Policeman (who has received a tip). 'YES, AN' YER CAN'T DO WITH 'EM!
IF YER 'OLLERS AT 'EM, THEY HONLY TURNS ROUND AND SAYS, "PIP, PIP"!'

[*Punch*, Oct. 1, 1898

A few years later bicycling was to become 'the thing' in London for the fashionable world, who would be driven down with their machines to exercise in Battersea Park; and *Punch* artists did not let that pass unnoticed, either.

1896 was, of course, the year of the Locomotives on Highways Act—'The Emancipation Act'—under which the speed limit was raised from four to twelve miles an hour, and the previous requirement that there should be a man with a red flag walking in front of the vehicle was lifted. *Punch* still treated the horseless carriage as a joke, and the occasional pictures or paragraphs concentrated on the funny costumes worn, the inevitability of breakdowns or loss of control, and the approaching disappearance of the horse—the only thing for which it would always be required, said *Punch*, would be for drawing bathing machines in and out of the sea! But, in 'a forecast of the Derby a few years hence' two horses are shown looking on at a Motor Derby which is being run by machines propelled by steam power, by paraffin or by electricity, and one says to the other: 'The machines require jockeys as much as we did —in fact, even more, because, you see, *we* had intelligence and did not work by machinery.'

All sorts of innovations were forecast—however laughably improbable they might have appeared at the time: houses on wheels, a motor bath chair, a motorized Lord Mayor's Carriage, and even a motor hunt, with electric or steam foxes as well as horses. Reminiscent of the well-known Victorian song, 'The Tin Gee-Gee', there was a picture, 'Signs of the Times in the Lowther Arcade', showing a wooden horse marked 'To clear: 9½d.' beside a toy motor car, 'Just out: 3/11'. It was even suggested that, for the safety of bicyclists, a man with a red flag should precede all horses in future.

The idea of Science in the Force was still a matter for facetiousness. Commenting on a paragraph in the press: 'The scientific burglar must be met, or better, perhaps, followed, by the ultra-scientific policeman', *Punch* had some verses in which Policeman X Junior says (in the uneducated jargon so often still attributed to him by humorous writers):

'Wot you want, to match a burglar, after all, gents, is a Man!
And the Perlice Force horganised on this new skientific plan,
With their pockets full o' batteries, and the new (Pleaceman) "X ray"
Up their sleeves, might look himposing, but I've doubts if it would pay!'

Judy had a picture of the 'Automaton', an electrically operated dummy policeman performing the functions of traffic-signal lights today. There were simple jokes about the mistakes which might arise when the police got the long-promised telephones;

AUTOMATON
[*Judy*, Dec. 2, 1896

[*Punch*, Dec. 17, 1898

while *Punch* had a drawing of a constable on point duty provided with a foot-warmer
to stand on.

Up to 1897 boots had been officially supplied to the police; now they were allowed
to purchase their own, receiving an allowance of 6d. a week to pay for them. *Punch*,
apparently misunderstanding the arrangement, had a cartoon of the Home Secretary
collecting the price of a pair of boots from each Bobby.

This was the year of the Diamond Jubilee. 'A Great Tour de Force' was the title of
a full-page cartoon, showing Mr. Punch shaking hands with a police sergeant and
thanking the Metropolitan and City police for all they had done in facilitating traffic
and preserving order on Jubilee Day. Another picture shows a pickpocket, jammed in
a crowd under the nose of a policeman's horse, saying:

> 'Squash! Why, s'elp me, if I ain't 'ad my 'and in this cove's pocket for the larst
> twenty minits, an' can't get it out!'

A presentation at Bow Street to a retiring Detective-Sergeant and the Chief
Magistrate's description of the virtues of the perfect policeman—'absolutely without
fear, gentle and mild in manner, utterly free from swagger'—inspired *Punch* to some
verses, after Wordsworth's 'The Happy Warrior':

> 'Who is the happy "Copper"? Who is he
> Whom every Man in Blue should wish to be?

It is the placid spirit, who, when brought
Near drunken men, and females who have fought,
Surveys them with a glance of sober thought.

The Perfect Bobby brings cool reason's test
To shocks and shindies, and street-blocking shows;
Men argue, women wrangle—Bobby *knows*!'

Trials with bloodhounds for manhunting in 1898 led to a picture of the rural policeman and the difficulties he might have in keeping up with them.

Q. E. D.

À propos of the trials of man-hunting by bloodhounds taking place in Yorkshire, and their use in tracing crime, supposing bloodhounds can run down criminals, where will the Policemen be!

[*Punch*, Oct. 8, 1898

At various stages of the Dreyfus trial that year—it was not concluded until the following year, when he was sentenced to ten years' imprisonment, to the general indignation*—*Punch* did not conceal its disapproval of the methods being followed in France. In October 1898, for instance, it printed 'Mr Punch's Dreyfus Dictionary' which included:

'JUGER (from the French), to juggle. Hence *chose jugée*, equivalent to an affair in which some juggling has taken place.

SCHWARTZKOPPEN. A copper (or kopper), vulgarly, means a policeman. Hence, to schwartzkop is to detect or expose, and when a story is shown to be false and ridiculous, it is said to be *schwartzkoppen*.'

* It is interesting to recall that a substantial factor in the subsequently discredited evidence was the positive identification of the handwriting by Bertillon, whose anthropometric system was shortly to be largely replaced by the evidence of fingerprints.

There was an amusing cartoon in 1899 showing constables variously attired as foreign interpreters for alien visitors—a foretaste perhaps of the helpfulness which was to make film stars from other countries say: 'I think your police are wonderful!'

That year saw the outbreak of the Boer War; but *Punch* seems to have noticed little change in life of the streets of London, although police forces were depleted by considerable numbers of Reservists who went back to their regiments, while numbers of omnibus horses were also requisitioned. Even the scenes on Mafeking night, which must have kept police very busy, inspired no special pictures. Nor had *Punch* anything to say about the official adoption of fingerprints at Scotland Yard in 1901, the year of Queen Victoria's death, and the accession of King Edward VII. A cartoon 'Bobs as Bobby' followed a suggestion that Lord Roberts should be appointed to the vacant office of Lord High Constable, in the Coronation Honours, and showed him in police helmet.

Another five or six years were to pass before *Punch* began to recognise the horseless carriage as something more than a rare curio: it was still always referred to as the 'new' motor-car, and figured only in occasional facetious drawings which concentrated on its liability to break down and require a horse to tow it home, or its propensity for running over dogs or chickens. But by 1903 they were envisaging 'the Motor Age'. That was the year of the Act of Parliament—the first statute in which the term 'motor-car' was used—which raised the speed limit to 20 m.p.h. and introduced registration number plates. *Punch* now tended to identify it with 'the moneyed classes' as enemies to the pedestrian, who it was even suggested might want to carry firearms to protect himself against motorists. The motor-cyclist, too, was now coming to be regarded as a new scourge on the roads. One picture in *Punch* shows two 'scorching cyclists' sitting by the roadside watching a motor-cyclist tear past. 'Call that exercise?' says one; to which his friend scathingly replies: 'No. I call it sitting in 'a draught.'

The police speed trap makes its first appearance in *Punch* pictures in 1902. Surrey—as a dormitory county, easily accessible from London for motor-cars with their short mileage—got more than its share of them. A recently appointed ex-army Chief Constable was determined on a strict enforcement of the law; already he regarded cyclists as a menace; now he spoke of the invention of the internal combustion engine as 'the greatest curse of modern civilisation'. (The press called it 'motorphobia'.) He opposed road widening as encouraging fast driving; and even then was advocating the creation of a separate body of traffic wardens. There was much the same attitude to the motor-car in most of the other Home Counties; much would depend on the personal views of the Chief Constables—some of whom were very elderly, having held their posts for thirty or forty years, and had their roots firmly embedded in the era of the horse. The younger constable might find it a little difficult at times to remember which side he was on—as the drawing illustrates. The mechanics of the automobile were still a bit

Sporting Constable (with stop-watch—on 'Police Trap' duty, running excitedly out from his ambush, to motorist just nearing the finish of the measured furlong). 'FOR 'EVIN'S SAKE, GUV'NOR, LET 'ER RIP, AND YE'LL DO THE 220 IN SEVEN AND A 'ARF!'

[*Punch*, Jan. 3, 1906

above the heads of some of the older men, of course: there is one picture of a bucolic policeman, taking down particulars from a motorist who has come back to his parked car to find the magneto missing, and saying: 'Now, Sir, would you be prepared to swear that you had it when you arrived?'

Scouts of the Automobile Association, which was formed in 1905, began warning their members when police traps were ahead. Early police prosecutions for 'aiding and abetting' failed, and *Punch* had cartoons showing the roadside crowded with signboards and people of all sorts giving every conceivable form of warning. Still siding on the whole with the pedestrian, they had one cartoon showing two policemen carrying a flattened-out body for treatment at the Pedestrians' Restoration Department, which they suggested should be included in the Motor Show of 1907 at Olympia; but by 1908 they were beginning to see both sides of the question. The full-page cartoon by

CONFLICTING INTERESTS; OR, JOHN BULL'S MOTOR PROBLEM

[*Punch*, Aug. 19, 1908

Bernard Partridge under the title 'Conflicting Interests, or John Bull's Motor Problem',
showed Bull in the dual capacities of pedestrian and motorist. That year the Surrey
police got convictions against A.A. scouts for obstructing the police; one was taken to
the appeal court, where the conviction was upheld. Thereafter there was more compromise between the A.A. and the police; and *Punch* fell back on humorous drawings

RID HIMSELF OF THE NUISANCE BY A SIMPLE AND INEXPENSIVE DEVICE

[*Punch*, March 30, 1910

such as one in which the motorist carried a dummy inspector in uniform in the front seat beside him, so that he would be saluted and allowed by the constable to pass, and another in which a resident, anxious to secure peace in his roadside garden, puts dummy policemen with stop watches at each end of the wall, looking over the top.

Though eight years were still to pass before Blériot's flight across the Channel really brought the 'heavier-than-air' machine into the public eye, *Punch* had a prophetic drawing of winged police of an Aerial Division as far back as 1901.

INCREASED ACTIVITY OF THE POLICE
A Possibility of the very near future
P.C. X. (of the A. or Aerial Division.) 'NOW THEN, THIRTY MILES AN HOUR WON'T DO
UP HERE! I'VE TIMED YOU WITH MY ANEROID BAROMETRICAL CHECK CLOCK, AND
YOU'LL HAVE TO COME DOWN TO THE STATION!'

[*Punch*, Nov. 6, 1901

In London and other big cities, up to 1914 the chief bugbear of the police in keeping the streets free of congestion had been the omnibuses and cabs. The replacement of the horse-drawn 'growler' and hansom by motor 'taxis' took rapid strides between 1907 and 1912; the 'growler', which had previously been summoned by one blast on the whistle, was ousted by the motor-taxicab in 1908, and now relegated to three. The

replacement of horse by motor-driven omnibuses became noticeable by 1906: the last
ran in London in 1916. A full-page cartoon by Bernard Partridge early in 1907,
entitled 'The Mammoth City of Din', shows an allegorical figure blocking her ears
against the blare of innumerable motor-horns.

The case of Adolf Beck—released in 1904 with a 'Free Pardon' after a second con-
viction on wrong identification—revived the question of a Court of Criminal Appeal.
Bernard Partridge had a full-page cartoon which showed the blindfolded Goddess of
Justice outside the Home Office, and 'Policeman X' saying to her:

> 'Court o' Criminal Appeal? You've got the 'Ome Office 'ere. Wot more do you
> want?'

To her reply 'I've tried that', he can only say

> 'Well, there ain't no other. Pass along, please.'

Three years later, when the Court of Criminal Appeal was created, another cartoon
showed an editor of the 'Yellow Press', robed as a judge, complaining that it would put
an end to re-trial by newspapers. An even more bitter cartoon shows the Gutter
Press, in the person of a depraved scavenger standing knee-deep in slime, with a poster
advertising 'FULL DETAILS OF THE HOME LIFE OF THE FEMALE PRISONER', holding out his
hat and calling out:

> 'Here you are, gents! Chuck us a few more coppers an' I'll *roll* in it!'

The passing of the first Aliens Act in 1905, and the Children's Act of 1908, all
interested *Punch*, who had several cartoons about each.

The Royal Commission on Police, which had been sitting and hearing evidence
since 1906, reported in 1908 giving the police a clean bill on the whole; and *Punch* had
a full-page cartoon, 'Pass Along, Please', showing all the calumnies and slanders against
the police creeping away.

The police constable was still generally pictured as a rather stolid worthy, with a
predilection for the rabbit pie offered him by the cooks or housemaids in the areas on
his beat.

A lesser-known chorus to the famous music-hall song goes:

> 'If you want to get a drink, ask a Policeman!
> He will manage it, I think, will a Policeman.
>   If the pubs are shut or not,
>   He'll produce the flowing pot.
> He can open all the lot, can a Policeman!'

PASS ALONG, PLEASE!

[The Police, after being examined on certain charges before a Royal Commission, have 'left the Court without a stain upon their character'].

[*Punch*, July 8, 1908

Cook. 'Now we've 'ad words, you'll be lookin' for another cook to keep company with?'

Policeman. 'Not me. I'll starve first!'

[*Punch*, March 27, 1907

A drawing in *Punch* in August 1914 shows a police sergeant smacking his lips over a pint mug at the back door of a pub after hours, disturbed by a patrolling constable who explains his presence:

'I heard an unusual sound, Sir.'

Another picture shows Bill Sikes, suddenly finding a policeman having a quiet smoke under a wall, pointing a pistol at him and saying: ' 'Ands up—both of 'em!' The constable, who has hastily put one hand holding the pipe behind his back, says: 'Sh! Don't talk so loud, yer fool! 'Ere comes the Inspector. You'll get us both into trouble!'

George Belcher had a drawing of a constable in argument with a loafer who, when told 'Now then, move on there, and don't make a crowd on the pavement,' protests: 'But two ain't a crowd.' The constable can only reply: 'One's a crowd, if I say so! Move on.' (Albert Chevalier's village constable had taken much the same line:

> 'Oi can't 'ave that, Oi sez, Oi can't.
> Ah! You may stand an' gi' Oi jaw,
> But when Oi sez a thing, Oi sez,
> The thing Oi sez be law!')

An Irish policeman in a drawing some years later tries to get to the bottom of the matter by explaining: 'Sure, if every wan was to stand in the wan place, how would the rest go by?'

There were some verses in 1908 worth quoting from:

> 'I'm always worried when I see
> The capes of Scotland Yard suspended
> Upon a lamp-post or a tree,
> Apparently quite unattended.
> It surely cannot be a trap
> To catch some water-proof-less chap?'

It was in 1906 that the militant suffragettes—dubbed by *Punch* 'The Shrieking Sisters'—really began to be troublesome. E. T. Reed had a cartoon of Herbert Gladstone (then Home Secretary in the new Liberal government) in police uniform, recalling the incident in Birmingham during the Boer War when Lloyd George, making pacifist speeches, had had to borrow a policeman's uniform to make his escape by a back door of the Town Hall from the fury of angry bloods. He had another showing a

H-RB-RT GL-DST-NE
[*Punch*, January 10, 1906

policeman carrying a hysterical suffragette from the Ladies' Gallery at the House of
Commons—where a debate on a Women's Suffrage Bill was being talked out. Asquith

SAFEST AND CHEAPEST TRAVELLING IN LONDON

New method of transit invented by our hysterical friends the Suffragettes; cheaper, quicker and
more reliable than tubes or motor-buses.

[*Punch*, May 2, 1906

(now Prime Minister) and Herbert Gladstone were caught by surprise by suffragettes on a golf course; and thereafter police bodyguards accompanied them as necessary—though probably not on the scale suggested in a full-page cartoon in September 1909. (Another drawing showed dozens of police, with magnifying glasses and bloodhounds, called to a golf links to help find a lost ball—it being the time of the rubber boom.)

If Cabinet Ministers must have six policemen in attendance when they play golf on Saturday afternoons, then each policeman might surely carry a club. This would serve a double purpose: (1) Caddies could be dispensed with; (2) The clubs would serve as weapons of offence and defence in case of a Suffragette raid.

[*Punch*, Sept. 22, 1909

The militant suffragettes were by now going in for window-breaking, incendiarism, and chaining themselves to railings. Ju-Jitzu had recently been taken up in this country, and the suffragette shown in the cartoon reproduced here had evidently anticipated the training of policemen in the art—though E. T. Reed had had another cartoon, showing three of the House of Commons police practising it with dummy suffragettes. Kipling's poem 'The female of the species is more deadly than the male' appeared in *The Times* in 1911.

THE SUFFRAGETTE THAT KNEW JIU-JITSU
The Arrest

[*Punch*, July 6, 1910

In February 1910 Winston Churchill, then thirty-six years old, became Home Secretary—and, it is recorded, personally tested the forcible feeding which had to be applied to suffragettes who hunger-struck in prison.

> 'Once a week, or perhaps oftener', Sir Edward Troup, then Permanent Under-Secretary at the Home Office, has written, 'Mr Churchill came down to the office, bringing with him some adventurous and impossible project; but after half an hour's discussion, something evolved which was still adventurous, but no longer impossible.'

One of his first duties was to pilot the Police Weekly Rest-Day Bill through the House. He stood firmly behind the police when they were criticised for the way they handled

WHEN CONSTABULARY DUTY'S TO BE DONE

Mr Lloyd George (*to the new Home Secretary*). 'I SUPPOSE YOU'RE GOING TO SETTLE DOWN NOW?'

Mr Winston Churchill. 'YES; BUT I SHAN'T FORGET YOU. IF YOU FIND YOURSELF IN TROUBLE I'LL SEE IF I CAN'T GET YOU A REPRIEVE, FOR THE SAKE OF OLD TIMES!'

[*Punch*, Feb. 23, 1910

the suffragettes under great provocation. Ever since he had entered Parliament ten years before, everything he did had attracted full attention in *Punch*, who christened him 'Winsome Winnie'; and now a full-page cartoon by Raven Hill, under the title 'When Constabulary Duty's to be Done', showed him—wearing the midget Homburg or trilby known as 'the Winston hat'—promising sympathetic consideration for Lloyd George (with whom his relations had been variable). They had been jointly interested

MR WINSTON CHURCHILL
LOSES HIS SHEPHERD
[*Punch*, June 7, 1911]

in the Dartmoor Shepherd who had had many convictions for robbing church offertory boxes: Winston Churchill decided to give him another chance—but he was back in prison before long. This lies behind the cartoon of Churchill as a Dresden Shepherdess in 'Punch's Illustrated Programme of Coronation Variety Turns'. The press generally were critical of his action in going down in person to supervise the Battle of Sidney Street; *Punch* confined its references to a few rather unkind allusions to the coincidence that press photographers were also there. The cartoons were giving attention to the inadequacy of control of undesirable aliens.

In 1911 members of Parliament first became salaried, at £400 a year. In November Churchill left the Home Office for the Admiralty; but he had stayed long enough to get the police a rise in pay which, though it would only have been a few shillings, justified 'Mr Punch's Warm Felicitations to the Force' and a cartoon showing one constable, holding a substantial bag of money in his hand, saying to another:

'Well, *we*'ve got a bit of extra pay, mate, "over and above" as you might say, and *not had to strike for it.*'

The period was one of much labour unrest and strikes; and *Punch* had a good deal of sympathy for police with 'the bottle-throwing hooligan—the worst enemy of Labour'. There is nothing new about 'unofficial strikes'. The Trades Disputes Act of 1906 had given Labour its charter for 'the right to strike'; but already by 1910 *Punch* had a full-page cartoon showing a Trade Union Official, left behind by the crowd, protesting: 'Steady on, there, wait for your leader! When I gave you that banner, *Down with Authority*, I didn't mean Down with *my* Authority!' Special constables to the number of eight thousand were sworn in—the first large recruitment since the Chartist and Fenian troubles of the middle of the last century. In another full-page cartoon, entitled 'Self-defence', John Bull, 'of the new Volunteer Police', wearing an

THE RIOTER'S IDEAL

[*Punch*, Sept. 10, 1913

armlet and carrying a truncheon, says to a Trades Union Leader: 'Look here, my friend, I've been hearing a good deal of talk of "recognition". Well, I represent the Public, and it's about time *my* interests were "recognised".'

Punch had only two pictures bearing directly on all the work of the police at the Coronation of King George V in 1911. One was a fanciful one arising from an order excluding aeronauts from the Coronation route. The other pays tribute to the way the humblest members of the public relied on the policeman to help them, and the good humour with which the police tried to comply.

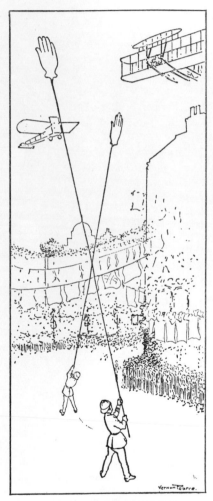

A suggestion to aid the Police in carrying out the recent order to exclude aeronauts from the Coronation route.

[*Punch*, June 7, 1911

Mrs Bucket. 'PREPS YOU WOULDN'T MIND TELLIN' ME WHERE 'UD BE ABAHT THE BEST PLACE TO SEE THE CORINATION?'

Policeman. 'WELL, I SHOULD SAY SOMEWHERE INSIDE THE ABBEY WOULDN'T BE ARF A BAD PLACE.'

[*Punch*, June 21, 1911

POLICEMAN ON POINT DUTY
[*Punch*, Nov. 8, 1911

A page of cartoons, based on the innovations in the ballet—where Nijinsky and Mordkin had shown that the male dancer can be manly though graceful—included amongst others two of policemen dancing through their duties.

POLICEMAN EFFECTING ARREST OF BACCHANAL
[*Punch*, Nov. 8, 1911

(Some doubt has been placed upon the reliability of Bernard Shaw's own story of how, returning late at night after seeing the ballet at the Alhambra, he had tried spinning round himself in Fitzroy Square (where he was then living). At his fourteenth fall he was picked up by a passing constable, whom he persuaded to try it with him. The visiting inspector, an early postman and a milkman—he has said—subsequently joined in.)

The problem of traffic control at 'fixed points' would still be largely a London one. Two pictures illustrate the ingrained habits which the policeman acquires—in one case, a London policeman on holiday in the country, in the other, a country policeman returning after a day in London.

FORCE OF HABIT
The London Policeman takes a holiday
[*Punch*, July 17, 1912

EXTRAORDINARY BEHAVIOUR OF A COUNTRY POLICEMAN AFTER A DAY'S VISIT TO LONDON

[*Punch*, Feb. 26, 1913

THE COMPLEAT POLICEMAN

(A new schedule has, we understand, been issued to the Force, entitled 'Hints for Police employed on Traffic Duty'.)

'THE REGULATION OF TRAFFIC, SO AS TO PREVENT OBSTRUCTION OR ACCIDENT, REQUIRES TACT.'

'NEVER GET FLUSTERED OR ANNOYED'

'KEEP A LOOK-OUT FOR THE CARRIAGES OF PRIVILEGED PERSONS.'

[*Punch*, **March 25, 1914**

By 1914, special instructions for police on traffic duty in the Metropolis had been issued, and inspired E. H. Shepard to some fanciful sketches.

Punch's issue for 5th August 1914 had gone to press too soon for any reference to the outbreak of war to be included; and—apart from two full-page cartoons in the issue of 29th July, showing war-clouds hanging over Europe—its pages remained light-hearted until 12th August. The Ulster crisis had been the most serious. Now the suffragette problem disappeared overnight, the Pankhursts and others turning all their energies at once to war work. An Aliens Act (already in draft) was passed on the 5th; it gave the first effective control over aliens in this country, and was to be continued after the war was over. The Zeppelin was the air-raider expected; and the cartoon by George Morrow echoes the general feeling of people at home that the policeman would still be their most trusted friend, as he was to be in the Second World War.

Perhaps the London public would feel more secure if our guardian airship
were made in this pattern

[*Punch*, Sept. 30, 1914

Of the regular police, large numbers of Army and Fleet Reservists were called up on the outbreak, while many others wanted to enlist. Special Constables had hitherto only been appointed when tumults or riots had actually taken place or were apprehended: a new Special Constables Act passed before August was out authorised their appointment and continued employment irrespective of immediate emergency; and applications poured in. There were the usual jokes, as there had been in the middle of the last century, of the timid amateur who can only say to the rough: 'Now, look here, if you don't clear off, I'll—I'll call a Policeman!' or of the street urchin who says: 'Garn, silly, frightenin' me—I thought it was a real Copper!' It was a form of voluntary work which many of the older members of the *Punch* staff would naturally undertake; and their efforts to copy Robert only increased their admiration for him, while showing them how greater a physical ordeal his daily tour of duty involved. Some verses ended:

'Tis perfectly plain that, although it
    Is easy to offer one's aid,
The P.C., alas! like the poet,
    Is born and not made.'

But their contribution to the guarding of vulnerable points was of course invaluable, as *Punch* was to recognise with a full-page cartoon before 1915 was out.

ON THE KING'S HIGHWAY

Special Constable. 'WHO GOES THERE?'
Mr Punch. 'A FRIEND OF ALL GOOD CITIZENS—AND VERY GRATEFUL TO YOU.'

[*Punch*, Oct. 13, 1915

With so many larger issues to claim first attention, it is not surprising that drawings about police appeared less frequently during the war years. Spy scares, lighting offences, breaches of food restrictions or using petrol for pleasure accounted for most. There was more than one picture of the rural constable interfering with an artist, whether because cloud effects might be of use to the enemy aeronautical department, or because he mistook cubist drawings for plans. The standing joke of the partiality of policemen for cooks took a new turn, with women leaving domestic service for munition work, and being replaced (if at all) by less attractive substitutes. The cartoon by Frank Reynolds

P.C. 'WHAT'S BECOME OF THE LITTLE 'OUSEMAID?'
The Latest Thing in Domestics. 'OH, SHE'S WORKING ON MUNITIONS. YOU'LL HAVE TO TALK TO ME NOW.'

[*Punch*, May 17, 1916

had had its parallel over thirty years earlier, when 'Policeman (who had been whistling down this Area all the morning) is greeted by a Chinaman who, in answer to his "Is the cook in?" says blandly: "Me am cookey!" '.

The role of village police constable remained, as in peace-time, very much a one-man job. There was one picture of the country doctor whose driver can't get the tail-light of the car to burn. 'Oh, never mind,' says the doctor. 'We're only going home, and I've got the constable safe in bed with lumbago!' Some pleasant verses by C. L. Graves on 'Our Village Policeman' appeared in 1917. The last is worth quoting here:

'He's more than a man; he's a part of the map;
His going would cause a deplorable gap;
And the village would suffer as heavy a slump
As it would from the loss of the old parish pump.'

Women voluntary patrols, with the co-operation of the police authorities, had been working since the very early days of the war. The only reference to women police which I can trace in *Punch* is under a picture which appeared in the summer of 1915, where a youth of the type then regularly dubbed 'slacker', 'shirker' or 'Cuthbert', is saying to his three lady companions: 'It's all very well to talk about Policewomen. But what could they do against us men?' and one of them promptly replies: 'I suppose the authorities think that they would be quite a match for those who remained at home.'

'Flag Days' came into general existence during the war, and by 1917 were becoming such a nuisance that Lewis Baumer had a drawing of police specially employed to regulate the crowds of men queuing to have flags stuck in their buttonholes by a pretty revue actress.

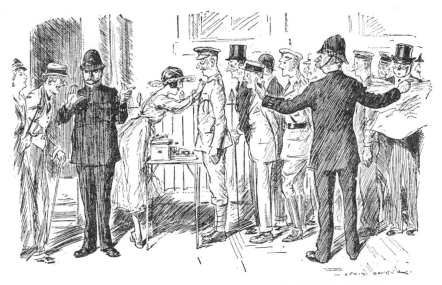

MISS DAISY DIMPLE, THE REVUE FAVOURITE, SELLS FLAGS.

[*Punch*, June 27, 1917

Eleanor Farjeon included 'Scotland Yard' in her series of whimsical 'New Nursery Rhymes of London Town'. 'How long's the Yard in Scotland?' she makes the girl ask her mother; and, on being assured that it is neither more nor less than the standard thirty-six inches, she complains:

> 'Then the bonny lad that sold me plaid
> Will never get to heaven.'

It was in the summer of 1916 that Bateman drawings began to appear in *Punch*. It is impracticable to include here the two full pages of drawings of 'Prisoner, when arrested, clung to the railings', the first in which police appear; I have selected five of the twenty to illustrate the start, the climax, and the dénouement of the story.

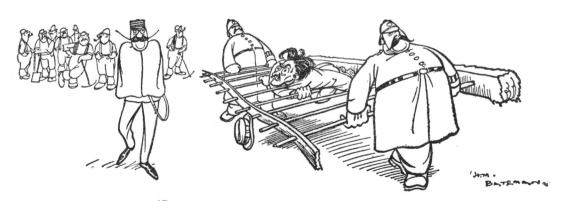

'PRISONER, WHEN ARRESTED, CLUNG TO THE RAILINGS.'

[*Punch*, Aug. 8, 1917

By 1918 the vagaries of the woman driver were becoming notorious. Two drawings by Stampa illustrate them. In one, the passenger says: 'You ought to have pulled up—the policeman waved his hand,' and the young woman replies: 'I never take any notice of their familiarity.' In the other, having charged the point-duty man in the back, 'Fair Chauffeuse' says:

> 'You're a very foolish man to stand in the middle of the road; it's lucky for you I happened to be looking and could pull up in time.'

[*Punch*, July 24, 1918

The idea of police going on strike has now faded into history and seems unrealistic; but in 1918 claims for improved pay had been outstanding too long, and 'the right to confer' was in dispute, although it had been actively canvassed since before the war. The strikes of 1872 and 1890 had been relatively small and short-lived. The strike of August 1918 involved the London police only, but 6,000 men came out. *Punch* confined its comments to two short paragraphs in 'Charivaria'.

> 'Seeing a large body of policemen strikers marching through New Bridge Street the other day, a dear old lady threatened to give them in charge.

> Owing to the fact that it was their busy season, it seems that the burglars were unable to come out in sympathy with the London police.'

There were no cartoons about Lloyd George's intervention, the resignation of the Commissioner of Police and the Home Secretary or the appointment of General Sir Nevil Macready as Commissioner.

There was an immediate increase of pay; but there were certain loose ends left; and now the provincial police were brought in. Another strike anticipated in May 1919 did not materialise; and *Punch* had a full-page cartoon, 'Faith Restored', and some verses by Owen Seaman, the editor, 'To Robert of the Force':

FAITH RESTORED

Mr Punch. 'STANDS ROBERT WHERE HE DID? GOOD! I WAS AFRAID FOR A MOMENT THAT MY IDOL HAD FEET OF CLAY.'

[*Punch*, June 11, 1919

'It was you who almost fell from grace,
Striking, like Lucifer, against authority,
Leaving your Heaven for another place
Not mentioned in your ten-to-one majority,
And doomed, to your surprise and pain,
Never, like Lucifer, to rise again.

To me I feel it would have mattered
Enormously to see my idol shattered.

If, tempted thrice, you break your trust,
You'll have no halo left to readjust.'

But hothead agitators were not satisfied, despite the fact that the desired improvements in pay and conditions of service were already promised; and a strike took place at the end of July. This time about a thousand of the 18,000 Metropolitan police withdrew their services; but so also did a number of the City police, five provincial police forces, and two prisons. All were dismissed, and *Punch* confined itself to a small cartoon 'All Quiet at Scotland Yard'. (Shortt was the name of the new Home Secretary.) The debates which took place in the House were unfortunately not reported in

ALL QUIET AT SCOTLAND YARD
'Shortt's the Friend.'

[*Punch*, Aug. 13, 1919

Punch's 'Essence of Parliament', though Pemberton Billing, Horatio Bottomley and a young man named Oswald Mosley, who were all Members at that time, doubtless gave scope for cynical comment.

Women having obtained the franchise in 1918, there was no more trouble with suffragettes. A revival of dog-muzzling regulations produced another cartoon in *Punch*.

PROTECT OUR PROTECTORS
Barbed wire-mesh overalls designed to prevent the police from striking as a protest
against having to intern unmuzzled dogs.
[*Punch*, May 14, 1919

The despatch of a small number of Metropolitan policemen to Warsaw to organise the police force there was the subject of a short paragraph in 'Charivaria':

'Whether they will ever master such difficult Polish phrases as "Youshutupyer-
jaw" or "Nunuvyerlip" is another question.'

12

The end of the year saw a debate in the House as to whether 'D.O.R.A.' (the much-maligned Defence of the Realm Act) should be extended into 1920; and a cartoon shows Bonar Law as a police constable regretting his inability to carry the old lady across the road.

Dora. 'DO YOU THINK YOU CAN GET ME ACROSS SAFELY?'

P.C. Law. 'SORRY, MUM, I'D HAVE LOVED TO CARRY YOU OVER, BUT I'M NOT ALLOWED TO.'

[Mr. BONAR LAW was refused permission to carry over the War Emergency Laws (Continuance) Bill to next Session.]

[*Punch*, Dec. 31, 1919

CHAPTER V

Between the Wars

THE whole status of the policeman was raised on the recommendations of Lord Desborough's Committee in 1919, the rates of pay of the constable becoming about three times what they had been before the war, and made standard for all forces. *Punch* seems to have let this pass without comment by cartoon or otherwise; but a reported speech by Sir William Gentle (retiring as chief of the Brighton police to play a leading part in the new business of greyhound racing tracks):

'Increased remuneration is attracting to the force a more intellectual and better class of recruit. A policeman is as much encouraged to prevent the necessity of an arrest as to effect an arrest',

inspired *Punch* to some verses, 'To the New Policeman':

'O Robert, in our hours of crime
Certain to nab us every time,

Discard your truncheon for a tract;
Strive to admonish ere you act;

Becoming a judicious blend
Of "guide, philosopher and friend";

In Virtue's force enrol recruits,
And stamp out Belial with your boots.'

Police recruiting had been in abeyance during the 1914–18 war, and many of the younger policemen had joined the armed forces. The end of the war consequently found all police forces short of establishments,* while there were many who, having stayed on beyond the pensionable ages, were now overdue to retire. Recruiting was immediately restarted and went on apace, largely from among demobilised men.

---

* The War Department and Admiralty had not yet founded their own Constabularies; and in 1920 there were still considerable contingents of London Metropolitan Police out-stationed at the principal dockyards, naval establishments and arsenals. The Metropolitan Police establishment was therefore 2,000 stronger than it is today; but the war had left them 3,000 short.

Many returned from commissioned rank to become constables, and were occasionally to find it embarrassing to meet war-time friends whilst on duty.

POLICE CONSTABLE (DEMOBILISED OFFICER) MEETS AN OLD
FRIEND FROM FRANCE

[*Punch*, Jan. 14, 1920

But the old idea of the policeman died hard. In 1923 *Punch* had a picture of the newly appointed rector of a country parish who, having been caught without a light on his bicycle, says: 'I say, our policeman's a sportsman. I gave him half-a-crown and he let me off!' to which the Squire and local J.P. replies: 'My dear fellow, you shouldn't do that—a shilling's ample!' The rural policeman of stage and fiction still appeared in some pictures.

Rural Sergeant. 'WHY, ONLY A FEW MONTHS AGO I 'ANDLED A VERY BIG CASE—A CASE O' CHICKEN-STEALING.'
  Visitor. 'BUT I DON'T CONSIDER CHICKEN-STEALING A PARTICULARLY BIG CRIME.'
  Rural Sergeant. 'AH, BUT IT WERE A BIG CASE. 'E PINCHED SEVENTEEN CHICKEN.'
                                    [*Punch,* Sept. 12, 1923

The Licensing Act of 1921 substituted 'permitted hours' for 'closing hours' in public houses (besides abolishing any concession to the *'bona fide* traveller'). A. P. Herbert in the Misleading Case of *Thomas* v. *Lowder: Lowder* v. *Thomas* a good many years later (where a constable, hearing voices in the bar after hours, had exercised his power of entry and been forcibly ejected: the licensee had issued a writ for the slanderous insinuation that drink might have been sold out of hours, while the constable had brought an action against the licensee for assault), was to make Mr Justice Plush, after giving the licensee heavy damages against the police, say:

> 'Loathsome though the provisions of the Licensing Act, 1921, must appear to any thinking citizen, that measure had one point of merit. It abolished what was known as "closing time". The sale and consumption of "alcohol", as it is called, can only take place within certain "permitted hours": but the inn need never be "closed".... This beneficent distinction should be more widely known than it is: and I hope that it will be impressed upon all young policemen.'

The Sinn Fein and I.R.A. troubles in Ireland at this time prompted a full-page cartoon 'Homage from the Brave', in which 'Old Contemptible' is saying to a member of the Royal Irish Constabulary:

> 'Well, mate, I had to stick it against a pretty dirty fighter, but thank God I never had a job quite like yours.'

Another full-page cartoon, on the disbandment of the R.I.C. in 1922, shows a member of the R.I.C. with his wife and children exiled from their home under threat of death at the hands of fellow-Irishmen.

Towards the end of 1921, the old trouble over the dual responsibility of the Assistant Commissioner of the Special Branch at Scotland Yard (then known as 'Director of Intelligence') had come to a head, and led to questions in the House. The main outline of the story can be read between the lines in 'Mr Punch's Essence of Parliament':

> 'Nov 3. Sudden departure of Sir Basil Thomson from New Scotland Yard. If Mr Shortt had been a little less curt in his method of satisfying Members' curiosity, but he refused to answer a straight question as to whether Sir Basil walked out or was pushed.
>
> Sir Reginald Hall, who from his experience as chief sleuth at the Admiralty paid tribute to Sir Basil's ability in diagnosing danger and frustrating plots before they developed, moved the adjournment.
>
> The Home Secretary explained that Basil Thomson did not get on with the new Chief Commissioner* and had always made it plain that he would resign if the

---

* Ever since 1855 there had been a single Commissioner of Metropolitan Police; but the title *'Chief* Commissioner', dating from the days of the original dual office, not infrequently appears even to this day.

Special Branch of the C.I.D. were placed under the direct control of General Horwood, and as that step had been decided upon "in the interests of efficiency", of course Sir Basil had to go. Much hostile criticism and indeed more damaging approval of the left wing.'

The situation was only saved by a threat from Mr Austen Chamberlain to resign; but the premature arrival at New Scotland Yard of an unacceptable successor, and interviews given to the press, brought the subject up again in the Commons, and 'Toby M.P.' commented a week later:

'The Home Secretary explained that Sir Basil Thomson enjoyed a certain independence of the Chief Commissioner. . . . General Horwood, who also appears to enjoy a limited independence of the Home Office, had not thought it necessary to inform him.'

1922 saw the introduction of Prohibition in the United States, on which *Punch*, commenting on an order that all policemen in New York must learn to swim, said:

'The idea is to use them for salving the empties in the neighbourhood of the three-mile limit.'

That year, Mr Shortt the Home Secretary appears in the guise of a uniformed P.C. with notebook, in a full-page cartoon about the Daylight Saving Bill, which was to make permanent the 'Summer-Time' introduced during the war. There were also some verses by Owen Seaman:

> 'Apparently it angers Hodge
>   To brush aside the morning dew;
> He loathes the Daylight Saving dodge;
>   His cow, it seems, dislikes it too;
> His sense of fitness it disturbs,
>   And hence the present case of *Rus* v. *Urbs*.'

The spread of interest in winter sports inspired a full-page drawing by Ernest H. Shepard, in which everyone is on skis or toboggans on Ludgate Hill, including the P.C. regulating traffic, who has caught the tip of his skis in the snow and fallen down.

It was in 1922 that Charlie Chaplin made his triumphal return visit to England, to be followed by Jackie Coogan, a boy prodigy of the American films, whom everybody seems to have been delighted to show anything.* (*Punch* even suggested the

---

* The then Commissioner of Police personally showed him round Scotland Yard, but was somewhat embarrassed by a riddle the precocious boy had been primed to spring on him:

'Say, Commissioner, why can you never get a policeman to pay his 'bus fare?'

Now this happened to be a rather controversial problem in London at the time; and the General was only partially appeased by the answer: 'Bekase you can't get nickel out of copper!'

unveiling of a tablet in Westminster Abbey, commemorating the fact that he had walked through the building.)

It was a time of many strikes, and *Punch* had a cartoon, 'A Too-Free Country', in which P.C. John Bull is shown arresting an Alien Rioter. The Special Constables Act of 1923—which made a permanent volunteer force of what hitherto could only be enrolled in times of emergency and had to be disbanded immediately the trouble was over—was resisted in the Commons by Labour members, who were convinced that the new 'Specials' were to be a sort of Fascisti and would be used as blacklegs and strikebreakers.

> 'In vain', says 'Toby M.P.', 'the Home Secretary pointed out that it was merely supplementary to the Act of 1831, and had no sinister object. . . . For his success he owed something to Mr Lansbury, who outdid all his previous achievements in mare's nesting by the discovery that the miniature rifle range at the Stock Exchange was for the purpose of training jobbers and brokers to shoot down strikers.'

A. P. Herbert, in an article reporting as an onlooker on 'A Little Riot in Trafalgar Square', said:

> 'The policemen have all put on civilian expressions to make the public think that nothing is going to happen. . . . Of course policemen's horses are never supposed to kick or to tread on one's toes. I know that. But do the horses know it?'

Police horses, it is well-known, are trained in a 'scare school' to be 'dog quiet' while men shout and cheer, wave flags, or make as many alarming noises as possible with rattles and trumpets, revolvers or back-firing motor engines; but there remains a suspicion in many people's minds that the horse is a large, clumsy and naturally vicious animal, which the rider cannot prevent from doing pretty much what it likes. *Punch* was to give something of the other side of the story in some verses which appeared in 1940.

> 'Is a police-horse ever fearful
>   As he bears against our paunches,
> Firmly pressing back our noses
>   With his massive polished haunches?
> Is a police-horse ever grateful
>   To the crowds with which he grapples
> For resisting the temptation
>   Of the pins beneath their lapels?'

One of the immediate post-war reforms was that of the Metropolitan Police mounted branch, which—though the Thames division, based on Colquhoun's Marine Police, generally claims this distinction—has the longest history, being the direct descendant of the Horse Patrol started by Sir John Fielding, the blind magistrate at Bow Street, two hundred years ago. Latterly the police horse had been what Sir Nevil Macready used to call the 'Carter Paterson' type of a Horse Artillery team—in contrast to the handsome spirited horses supplied by Tillings for the Metropolitan Fire Brigade of pre-war days (though in some provincial forces the same police horse might be used to draw fire engines, patrol wagons and 'Black Marias'). Such horses were useful enough for crowd control, but at a disadvantage in mobility at busy traffic jams. Cartoonists invariably depicted 19-stone policemen mounted on Clydesdales.

Now Lieut.-Col. Percy Laurie, D.S.O., of the Scots Greys, was brought in to the newly created rank of Deputy Assistant Commissioner to reorganise the mounted branch of the Metropolitan Police on the principles of a cavalry regiment. He personally bought light horses of the hunter type 'off the grass' from their breeders on Yorkshire farms. The drawing of 'Ingenuous Maiden' at the Derby gives some idea of the new

AT THE DERBY
Ingenuous Maiden (gazing at the Police mounts). 'I WONDER WHICH IS THE FAVOURITE.'
[*Punch*, June 13, 1923

type of police horse. The days were past when Surtees' Facey Romford could say he 'wouldn't mind being a chief constable, if they would let him hunt his horse occasionally'—but the chief constable of a county constabulary could still make time to hunt one day a week, and it might be convenient to keep his official mount in the same stables as his own horse.

Lord Trenchard, for all the drastic changes he made when he became Commissioner, was to lose no time in stating that he intended to retain the mounted police, not only for their value in marshalling processions and controlling disorderly crowds, but also for the advantage which height gave the policeman directing traffic at busy points. Today there are some 400 mounted policemen, half of them in the Metropolis; about

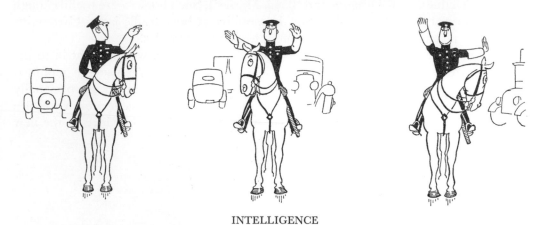

INTELLIGENCE

[*Punch*, Nov. 23, 1932

a score of the 123 other police forces in England and Wales still use horses, mainly in the industrial cities.

There is always a long waiting list of applicants for transfer to mounted duties. Most of them in the old days were men with previous service in the cavalry, gunners or yeomanry, or private service as grooms; but six months at the training school opened in the early 'twenties at Imber Court, Thames Ditton, could make a horseman from scratch. (In the 'twenties, there was a very senior police official who had recently come to Scotland Yard from the Navy, where horsemanship had not been part of the curriculum. Finding that he would be expected to appear on a horse on state occasions, he had set out to master the craft, and could be observed in the Row, morning after morning, sandwiched between two stalwarts of the mounted police, who were ready to salvage him if he fouled his anchor on either the port or starboard sides.)

Punch had a full-page picture of 'The Wild and Woolly West End' after the mounted police had taken part in the Royal Tournament at Olympia in 1922; but nothing about the scenes at the first Football Cup Tie Final at Wembley in April 1923, when the gates were rushed and tens of thousands of people swarmed over the playing pitch, and foot police were swallowed up by the human torrent, while the band played on. It was not until mounted men forced their way into the arena that control was regained: one man on a grey, known thereafter as 'Wellington of Wembley', brought order out of confusion; he was a late trumpet-major of the Royal Scots Greys, who had only been two years a policeman.

THE WILD AND WOOLLY WEST END

Showing the possible effect of the performance of the mounted police at Olympia on the manners of the force.

[*Punch*, June 28, 1922

'Imperial', the chestnut at present ridden by H.M. the Queen at Trooping the Colour parades, is provided by the Metropolitan Police, as was 'Winston', another chestnut chosen for H.M. King George VI, and immortalized on the crown pieces struck for the Coronation. But perhaps the most famous was Colonel Laurie's own army horse, 'Quicksilver', a grey, which he rode at the Police Centenary Parade in 1929 and the Royal Review of Police in Hyde Park in 1935. He 'went to grass' with his master in 1936, and was put down in 1943, rising 34 years old. 'Peccavi' wrote of him:

> 'Never a better, never a gamer,
> Never a truer friend.
> The *fun* we had together,
> The hours we used to spend!
> Sharing the joy of life to the full,
> Sharing the bad times, too:
> I might be disappointed in men,
> I was never let down by you.
> I never had a stauncher mate,
> And never a straighter pal,
> And as long as I'm on this earth, little chap,
> I know that I never shall.'*

In early days, the horseman was used to take urgent papers; in due course he would be succeeded for that duty by a policeman on a bicycle. Right up to 1914, few forces had any motor-cars—perhaps one for the chief officer; superintendents were driven from station to station in traps. After the war, motor-cars, motor-bicycles with side-cars, and motor-tenders were introduced. The spread of motoring was to bring the police the biggest addition to their work problems. In the 'twenties came the cheap light car—the 'baby Austin', the Morris Cowley and then the Ford 8. In the Commissioner's Annual Report for 1919 there were only ten lines devoted to 'traffic' as such: soon it was occupying many pages of a much bulkier booklet. Up to then transport had been a subject dealt with by one branch of the Board of Trade: now the Ministry of Transport was created, and a separate traffic department was formed at Scotland Yard for the first time.

The war had seen women and girls entering the field of 'automobilists'. There were many humorous drawings in *Punch* in the 'twenties of the lady driver.

'I say, this *is* a ridiculous waste of time', the young woman held up for scorching complains to the country P.C. taking down her particulars. 'I gave all the facts to a policeman ten minutes ago.'

* Reprinted by permission from *Horse and Hound*.

HAVEN

[*Punch*, Dec. 10, 1930

Another constable, asking a flapper driver to let him see her licence, gets the smiling reply:

'Ah, this is where you get stung. I'm too young to have one!'

The Delinquent (explaining). 'THEN I TROD ON THIS LITTLE GADGET AND IT SEEMED TO DO SOMETHING TO THE WHAT-YOU-MAY-CALL-IT. I *HOPE* I'M NOT BEING TOO TECHNICAL FOR YOU?'

[*Punch*, May 7, 1930

There is the young woman who reassures her uncle sitting beside her: 'No, I never worry about the speedometer. I just go by the coppers' faces.' There is the fair culprit who tells the constable, reading over what he has written: 'Monica Daphne Carmichael Haddington. Is that right?' 'Quite right—and just "Toots" to my friends.' And there is the more practical policeman who, having got down Christian names as far as 'Aloysius—Alistair—Cyprian—' puts his notebook away and says: 'Well, don't let me catch you again.'

By 1923 'Toby M.P.' was reporting:

'Mr Moore-Brabazon's assertion that the modern policeman had lost his knack of regulating traffic received hardly any support from other members. Labour and Toryism were for once unanimous in praising Robert's undiminished efficiency as a conductor of "the orchestral Strand".'

WANTED—A TRAFFIC AUTHORITY

John Bull. 'MY DEAR ROBERT, YOU'RE A MARVEL AT STOPPING THE TRAFFIC.'
Policeman X. 'THANK YOU, SIR; BUT WHAT YOU WANT IS SOMEONE TO KEEP IT MOVING.'

[*Punch,* July 11, 1923

Omnibuses and trams were generally held to be the basic cause of the congestion
in the principal thoroughfares of London. In 1924 Sir Samuel Instone put forward a
scheme for the revival of the steamboat service up and down the Thames, which has been
described as 'London's main highway'; but the L.C.C. refused to play, on the ground
that they could not risk the expense of reconditioning the piers. In a full-page cartoon
Mr Punch reminds them that they could apparently afford to risk loss on trams, which
helped to create the traffic blocks. (It was another thirty years before the last electric
tram ran in London.)

The traffic census by the mid-'twenties showed as much as 60% increase over the
pre-war volume of traffic at certain busy points in London. The number of private
motor-cars registered in Great Britain had already grown from 132,000 pre-war to
half a million. (The million mark was passed in 1930.) Mechanically drawn goods
vehicles had grown from 82,000 to a quarter of a million. Horse traffic still accounted
for 11% of the total in London, though the Beaverbrook Press was urging that it should
be banned altogether from goods transport in busy streets. The numbers were to go
down steadily, year by year, until now they represent only a tiny fraction of 1%;
and the stopping of runaway horses, or sitting on the head of a horse which had fallen
down between the shafts on the muddy roads, no longer figures in the policeman's
almost daily work.*

The year 1924 saw the passing of the London Traffic Act, with a London and Home
Counties Traffic Advisory Committee whose jurisdiction extended over an area three
times larger than the Metropolitan Police District. The Minister could now make Orders
for the co-ordination of road repairs: thirty-seven separate bodies had hitherto been
free to dig up London streets as and when they liked. Regulations now gave statutory
authority for the first time for leaving cars parked for prescribed periods in prescribed
places. The omnibus problem was alleviated by fixing stopping places compulsorily,
and prescribing approved routes, which put a check on the rivalries of competing
omnibus proprietors. (The London Passenger Transport Board was not created until
1933.)

Traffic duties were taking a great many policemen off their ordinary work. There
was a full-page cartoon by Bernard Partridge, 'The Mote and the Beam; or, the
Preoccupations of Scotland Yard', in which two burglars are shown picking the lock
of a jewellers' shop, while the constable in the background is taking down particulars
of a car left parked where it ought not to be; and one says to the other:

'We're all right; 'e's too busy tickin' off that car to notice us.'

Hardly a week passed without at least one humorous drawing of a motorist being ques-
tioned by a policeman, usually over a speed offence. The motorist is generally prepared

---

* The self-propelled vehicle created new problems in enforcing old Acts in which the use of the horse was
taken for granted. As late as 1960 the Court of Appeal had to decide the question 'Can you read "a motor-car"
for "a horse"?' in interpreting questions of expenses under the income tax rules.

P.C. 'You were doing forty miles an hour, Sir.'
Motorist (*whispering*). 'Make it seventy; I'm trying to sell him the thing.'
[*Punch*, Aug. 31, 1927

to treat the constable as a friend and ally—like the one who whispers (so that his passenger shall not hear): 'Make it seventy; I'm trying to sell him the thing.' Or there

TRAFFIC CONFUSION CAUSED BY CONSTABLE HAVING ASSUMED A
NEW AND RATHER TICKLISH UNDERVEST.
[*Punch*, April 22, 1925

is the argumentative motorist who, challenged with the allegation that he was doing forty miles an hour, replies:

'I can give you ocular demonstration that at half that rate this motor-car would fall to pieces.'

But the policeman must be no respecter of persons. To the celebrity, stopped for exceeding the speed limit, who demands: 'Don't you know who I am?' the constable promptly replies: 'No, and I'll want your address as well.' The pompous woman in a Rolls Royce who says indignantly: 'But you *must* know my husband; he gave away the prizes at the police sports!' gets the stolid reply: 'Ho, did he? Well, he never give *me* one!' On the other hand, the constable's dry sense of humour comes out now and then. 'I was hurrying to see my solicitor,' one motorist excuses himself. 'Well, we shall have some more news for him now,' the P.C. tells him. Likewise, when the doctor, held up for speeding on his way to an urgent case, protests: 'But for you, I'd be at the hospital now,' the constable replies: 'You would!'

Extremely zealous Officer. 'You can't come in this way.'
[*Punch*, Aug. 22, 1928

1925 saw the first gyratory or 'roundabout' traffic system tried out in Aldwych, and the introduction of one-way traffic down Haymarket and up Lower Regent Street. 'You can't go there, Miss; it's a one-way street,' one of George Belcher's police constables is shown telling a lady driver; to which she replies: 'But I only *want* to go one way!'

That year also saw the first white lines painted on the roadway at dangerous bends, soon to be replaced by aluminium studs; and the introduction of white gauntlets and gloves for the policeman on fixed traffic point duty. On the Home Secretary in the House declining a proposal that the traffic police should be put into white overalls, 'Toby M.P.' comments: 'He is right! If we dress Robert up as an umpire, he may think he is one. Far too many pedestrians are being given out "leg before" as it is.' A few weeks later, when the Home Secretary had told Members that devices for making traffic-policemen luminous at night had not been found satisfactory, the comment was: 'The difficulties will no doubt be overcome, and we shall have a Bill in Parliament before long requiring all traffic-policemen to be lit half-an-hour after sunset.'

It was a few years later that a proposal to fix a red lamp on the backs of traffic pointsmen after dark inspired 'Dum-Dum' to some verses:

> 'If he were picked out round his manly torso
>   With fairy-lamps, th'effect would be sublime,
> Like Brighton pier in summer, only more so,
>   Or some dream-palace in an Eastern clime;
> And, topping all, a clock with faces four, so
>   That, without asking, we could tell the time;
> That in a general way would be more like,
> And no one could mistake him for a bike.'

Life was certainly becoming more dangerous for the pedestrian.

About this time standardised traffic signals were being prescribed for all forces. Up to then, there had been a certain amount of variation according to common sense and individual discretion, and there were various pictures showing drivers in doubt what they were expected to do. There was, for instance, the wife saying to her hesitant husband at the wheel: 'Go on, Oscar. I think he really means it'; and the constable who asks the driver: 'Now what d'ye suppose I held me hand out for?' and gets the reply: 'Haven't the faintest. Often do it myself,' or the other who asks the lady driver: 'Wot yer stopping for?' to which she replies: 'Well, I noticed you bent your knees an' straightened 'em again. What signal was *that*?'

Solicitous Husband (in traffic). 'BE CAREFUL, DEAR!'
[*Punch*, June 10, 1925

DIFFERENT CARS, DIFFERENT SIGNALS

THE SIGN THAT WILL STOP A
MOTOR-OMNIBUS—

CAN EASILY BE PASSED UNNOTICED
BY A MIDGET 7—

SO WHAT IS REALLY WANTED—

IS A LITTLE ADAPTABILITY—

OR AN ENTIRELY NEW—

SET OF SIGNALS.

[*Punch*, Aug. 20, 1930

On the subject of motor-bicycles and the noise they made, Owen Seaman had some verses, addressed to the police generally, under the title 'The Curse of the Countryside':

'If in your exacting tasks
    You suffer from superfluous vigour,
Why don't you work it off, one asks,
    By carrying out, in all its rigour,
The Law forbidding hogs to raise
Hell on the King's highways?

O Robert, you who should deter
    The "mokist" from these foul abuses,
You who should be his silencer
    When he ignores that gadget's uses,
Why don't you lift your hand to stop
His pestilent pop-pop?'

An exhibition at Burlington House in 1929 of the Dutch Masters produced a full-page drawing by Ernest H. Shepard in which everybody, including the policeman regulating traffic, wore the clothes of the period.

MANNERS AND MODES
Showing the influence of the Dutch Masters at Burlington House.
[*Punch*, Jan. 16, 1929

I am not sure how early in the decade the 'Bright Young People' got that name: *Punch* had become aware of it by 1927. Innovations or phases of the 'twenties, round which many of the humorous drawings centred, included the dancing craze, supper and tea dances and the 'lounge lizard', syncopation and the memorable tunes of Irving Berlin and Jerome Kern and George Gershwin and Cole Porter and Ivor Novello and Noël Coward, the hobble skirt, bobbed or shingled hair, the cloche hat, the 'beaver' game, the crossword puzzle, and the collection of cigarette cards—besides dirt-track racing and the 'tote' and all-in wrestling, and the Flapper Vote. Several times *Punch* artists imagined the police constable's uniform adapted to the current fashions—anticipating the open-neck collar by at least twenty years.

THE VOGUE FOR SPATS

[*Punch*, April 19, 1922

THE 'CHARLIE'

[*Punch*, May 10, 1922

THE CLOCHE HAT
[*Punch*, March 12, 1924

NO MORE TIGHT COLLARS
[*Punch*, Aug. 15, 1928

A HYGIENIC YET A DIGNIFIED UNIFORM FOR POLICEMEN
[*Punch*, Aug. 30, 1933

And then came the wireless. An article by E. V. Lucas entitled 'The New Inqui-
sition', on the subject of a Bill which would empower police to enter houses in search
of illicit crystal sets or unpaid wireless licences, accompanied a full-page drawing in
which the cook, told by 'Indignant Householder': 'I am sorry to have to tell you that
we are liable to a visit from the police at any moment,' replies with a broad grin: 'Lor,
Sir, how lovely!'

The old 'rabbit-pie' joke was dying out, if only because there were fewer basement
kitchens, and domestic servants were becoming more independent and self-important;
but there were still quite a lot of them, and the young policeman was less of a 'type'
and had more to talk about. (That decade saw the old mews stables being converted
into garages, and the coachman's quarters over them becoming flats for the smart
set.)

'WHAT WAS THE FINEST DEED YOU EVER SAW?'
'AS TO THAT, MY LIPS IS SEALED, SEEIN' AS 'OW I DONE IT MYSELF.'

[*Punch*, Nov. 23, 1932

Psycho-analysis in relation to the criminal first appears in *Punch* in 1923, in some verses apologising to Freud for views expressed by Mr Justice Darling.

'For Darling, abruptly resigning
    The *role* of the jester, affirms—
Without hesitation defining
    His views in implacable terms—
That pleas for relief that are found in
    Sub-conscious temptations are banned
As having no warrant or ground in
    The Law of the Land.

At a time when supreme self-expression
    Is hailed as the ultimate good,
Such freaks of judicial aggression
    Must firmly be checked and withstood;
Or else we shall sink by swift stages
    Until we at last re-enact
The scenes of the barbarous ages
    When children were smacked.

No, no; all the stars in their courses
    Are fighting to help and to heal,
With other impalpable forces
    To whom we address our appeal:
Come down, then, unmoved by this snarling,
    This petulant carping at crime—
Come down, and redeem us from Darling
    O Spirit of Slime!'

A suggestion in 1926 by Sir Leonard Dunning, one of H.M. Inspectors of Constabulary, that 'the pantomime and the comic paper' idea of the policeman tended to keep some acceptable candidates from coming forward, inspired C. L. Graves to some verses, 'To Robert':

'You are not perfect, O my Robert—yet,
    Instead of inconsiderately railing,
Punch testifies that as a rule you set
    A high example of alert, unfailing,
Judicious zeal; that seldom you forget
    To help the very young, the old, the ailing;
And so he greets you, stout and genial warder,
    Best of our barriers against disorder.'

A few months later, after the General Strike, he had another set of verses, entitled
'Robert the Angel':

> 'O Robert in our hours of ease
> The butt of many an idle wheeze
> And subject to the chaff and jibes
> Of fractious and facetious scribes—
>
> In times of civic stress and strife
> When nerves are jarred and rumours rife,
> When care writes wrinkles on the brow,
> A blessing and a boon art thou.
>
> Bland, comfortable and benign—
> Unlike the fretful porcupine—
> You managed to diffuse the balm
> And solace of infectious calm.'

In spite of the stoppage of newspapers, there was no break in the issues of *Punch*
that May, although three numbers were restricted in set-up and circulation. A month
later there was a cartoon of the Home Secretary as a police constable, still enforcing the
Emergency Regulations. Meanwhile there had been a full-page cartoon by Raven

P.C. Jicks (*to Master Wedgwood Benn*). 'PASS ALONG THERE!
AND DON'T YOU DARE TO INTERFERE WITH ME IN THE EXERCISE
OF MY DUTY.'

[*Punch*, June 23, 1926

Hill of Mr Punch thanking the great army of amateur workers who had sustained the Nation's life on emergency services. A. P. Herbert had a cynical article, headed 'Fraternity', on what he saw after boarding an omnibus manned by volunteer driver and conductor.

'Perfect order had prevailed throughout, it seemed; the bricks thrown through the bus windows had been thrown in a most peaceful manner, and the engines smashed with the utmost gentleness, while in some cases the petrol-tanks had been ripped up with a movement that was almost a caress. One bus had been burned but without the smallest disturbance or ill-feeling; the driver of another had been taken off to hospital after being knocked about the face and body in a peacefully persuasive way. . . . I walked on mildly wondering what contribution this had made to the adjustment of the wages question in the coal-mines of South Wales.'

'Toby M.P.' reported how the Home Secretary had explained, in reply to an M.P.'s story of a 'terrible and unprovoked mass attack by constables, regular and special, on a number of his constituents harmlessly engaged in playing games', that the 'inoffensive citizens' were strikers who had violently assaulted a Special and stoned the police who came to his rescue.*

Anthony Armstrong put his regular *Punch* characters Percival and Apple on Special Constabulary duty and describes 'Exercise No. 1': Percival bends and straightens his knees, then inserts his thumbs in his mackintosh belt and with the out-stretched fingers of each hand pats his tummy three times in a judicial manner. Finally he slides his hands to and fro along the belt—and picks up his armlet which has fallen off. A small boy laughs. 'Now then, move along there,' says Percival. 'Shan't,' says the boy. Percival is not quite certain how he stands legally: finally he solves the problem by giving 'the crowd' sixpence, and the crowd disperses joyfully.

C. L. Graves had some more verses, 'Robert of the White Arm', in the following year:

'Help and advice gratuitously lending,
Showing a patience that no trial wearies,
Answering with grave tolerance unending
    Frivolous queries.

Punch, in old numbers, pictured you as stupid,
Plantigrade, moving always at a saunter,
Fond of your meals, a sort of kitchen Cupid,
    Area-haunter.

---

* It is a fact that, during the General Strike, an inspector was much more liable to assault than a helmeted constable, his flat cap being mistaken for that of a Special Constable, whom the strikers chose to regard as blacklegs.

Now he knows better, to the view inclining
That at a pinch you with the best can hustle,
Sturdy, athletic, happily combining
        Brains with your muscle.

Best, in Life's daily round, of problem-solvers;
Strong with the might that once the Red Cross Knight armed,
Chivalry, justice—better than revolvers,—
        Robert the white-armed.'

Punch still hardly noticed the women police. In 1921 a full-page cartoon depicting the various new occupations open to women had included a small figure of a woman constable. Miss Ellen Wilkinson in introducing a private Bill in 1925 requiring Municipal Corporations to appoint women police, explained (according to 'Toby M.P.') that there was no intention of exposing the burglar peacefully engaged in burgling or the coster engaged in jumping on his mother, to the rigours of the deadlier sex. A few years later there was an 'Ode upon the Police Force as a Profession for University Women':

'Hence, vain deluding female frills!
And, at the same time, drapers' bills;
With heart-felt joy I see
The uniform is free.

Hearing the sound of jocund glee
The mistress may not this time see
Behind the kitchen-door
(As always heretofore)

Cook entertaining P.C. Green,
But James the butler, smug of mien,
Pressing the best Chablis
On Miss Brown, B.Sc.'

1928 saw the opening of a proper Press Bureau at Scotland Yard. General Macready, who had had some experience of newspaper correspondents when he had been in South Wales during the coal strike in 1910 and in Ulster in 1914, had appointed the first 'press official' when he came to New Scotland Yard; but that officer, his private secretary, had only functioned as such during office hours. Now Lord Byng reorganised the press bureau service, with four press officers working as a team to cover a seven-day week until midnight at least, with an improved press room for reporters to wait in.

'The Press,' as Sherlock Holmes remarked rather bitterly to Watson, 'is a most valuable institution, if you only know how to use it.' Every police chief knows the difference between 'a good press' and 'a bad press'. Police news is always 'hot', and reporters are only interested in one point: 'Does it make a good story?'

COPS AND COPY

Press Reporter. 'I'VE GOT THAT DOWN: "IT IS CONFIDENTLY EXPECTED THAT AN ARREST WILL BE MADE TO-NIGHT IN THE SOUTH-EASTERN DISTRICT." I SAY, WHAT *would* YOU DO WITHOUT ME?'

Representative of Scotland Yard. 'THE OBLIGATION IS MUTUAL.'

[*Punch*, Oct. 12, 1927

But the job of the newspaper editor is not easy. An article in *Punch* pointed out how, even with a headline like 'Alleged Drunkard Kicks Alleged Policeman' you may be guilty of libel through excessive anxiety to avoid it.

'What a sensation a newspaper might make by avoiding the sensational!' A. P. Herbert wrote. 'Instead of STARTLING DEATH DRAMA. AMAZING REVELATIONS we should have SMALL MURDER. UNINTERESTING CRIME.

A very ordinary little murder was committed yesterday in Surbiton. We hesitate to draw our readers' attention to an event so trivial and fatiguing, but as a matter of record we are bound to say that last night the bodies of a mother and four children were found dead in a barn. There is no mystery about the case, the motive is obvious, and no further developments are expected. We hope we shall not have to refer to this tiresome homicide again.'

The 'twenties saw the beginning of the spate of fictional detective stories (though Penguins and similar paper-back editions were yet to come). There was a picture in *Punch* in 1925 of a bachelor uncle making a brave effort to entertain his small niece; but he has not got beyond 'Who Killed Cock Robin? I, said the . . .' before she interrupts him: 'Oh don't, Uncle—crimes bore me so.' *Punch* was many times to comment on the omni-presence of Edgar Wallace,* who wrote or dictated 150 books, hundreds of short stories and a score of plays. His principal character was J. G. Reeder, a semi-amateur who had however a room in the Public Prosecutor's department; but he also drew a real-life detective in Sgt. W. Arbuthnot Challenor, whose friendly contacts with the underworld were through Educated Evans the street tipster. Sir Basil Thomson, the Assistant Commissioner of the C.I.D., after his retirement was to debunk the cocksure amateur in the Mr Pepper stories. But with the notable exception of Freeman Wills Crofts' Inspector French, most of the fictional detectives of the 'twenties were still inspired amateurs like Holmes, showing up the 'official detectives' as painstaking but unimaginative and obtuse, to serve as convenient foils to the amateur's brilliance. 'Ours is the only trade in which the professional is always supposed to be wrong,' as G. K. Chesterton made Inspector Bagshaw complain to Father Brown. The provincial Chief Constable was generally depicted as a 'blimpish' retired regular army colonel; and the Scotland Yard Inspector who happened to be on holiday in the district was liable to go into the local police station and say: 'I think this will be a bit too much for you: I'll take it over.'

* I heard the late Lord Birkenhead, guest of honour at a C.I.D. dinner, finish a brilliant speech by telling his hosts:

'My friend Edgar Wallace and I have quite decided what we are going to do when we retire. We are going to form a private enquiry agency; and when any of you gentlemen are stumped, you need only come to us and we shall solve your problems for you. Just one thing is holding us up: we *cannot* agree whether the firm should be called "Birkenhead and Wallace" or "Wallace and Birkenhead"!'

'You bring on the local inspector of police', wrote A. B. Cox (*alias* Anthony Berkeley),

'and in due course the man from Scotland Yard. As is well known, this latter must be every sort of imbecile concentrated in one person. It is his practice when investigating a case to make every conceivable blunder that it is humanly possible for him to perpetrate. He is also extremely touchy, very conceited, and utterly contemptuous of the efforts of everybody but himself. If he were not all these things, your own amateur detective would not be able to score off him nearly so overwhelmingly in the end. Now no short story Inspector has ever been known to arrest the right man. The reader therefore at once knows that, whoever may have committed the crime, at any rate the person arrested did not do so. This narrows the field by one.'

There was a drawing by Charles Grave in 1928 in which the small burglar says to the plain-clothes officer taking him along to the police station:

'Blimey! I wish you was in love wiv my sister, same as in the detective stories.'

(He must obviously have been a student of Dorothy Sayers' Lord Peter Wimsey or Margery Allingham's Albert Campion while they were passing through their lovesick phases.) Some years later there were some verses, headed 'Where Should We Be Without Crime?'

> 'An author may vex with a treatise on sex
>   And induce the rebuffs of the parson,
> But he'll never disgust if he grants us our lust
>   For blackmail and murder and arson.
> So raise up your glass to the criminal class
>   And show them your grateful affection,
> For if they abode by the recognised code
>   There wouldn't be any detection.
>
>   Where should we be without crime?
>   Where should we be without Vice?
>   What would we do if the people we knew
>   Were all unbelievably nice?
> Who can imagine Lord Beaverbrook's fate
> If Europe's affairs were all run on the straight?
> And wouldn't Sir Philip's existence be tame
> If wrong 'uns decided to give up the Game?*
>   What would become of Miss Sayers
>   If everyone kept "on the level"?
>   I hope I am wrong, but I think before long
>   That *Lord Peter* would go to the Devil.'

* Sir Philip Game was Commissioner of Metropolitan Police at the time when this appeared in *Punch*.

H. F. Ellis in an article in *Punch's Summer Number* for 1938 on a 'Model Detective Story' could still say:

> 'Timothy Weybridge, famous criminal investigator and still popular as a week-end guest in spite of the nineteen murders which had occurred at the last dozen country-houses he had visited . . . rings up his old friend, Detective-Inspector Arthur Crabtree of The Yard, who happens by a fortunate chance to be staying at Castle Mannington, less than three miles away. They crack a few jokes together, for both are men of culture, and finally arrange that Crabtree shall fix things up with the Chief Constable . . . There should also be a chapter or two exhibiting Inspector Crabtree's tact in dealing with the local Superintendent. This shows acute knowledge of police procedure, and is never omitted. Students should note that Superintendents are heavyish, red-faced, quickly mollified men, with blue eyes that can on occasion become remarkably shrewd. Chief Constables should be kept in the background. They tend to say: "Carry on, then, Superintendent," rather testily when their arrangements for a day's rough shooting are disturbed. . . . A final solution so baffling and so utterly unexpected that even the author has to read it through three times before he can believe his eyes.'

But by the 'thirties the country house murder case was less often being handled by the amateur sleuth or opinionated dilettante. The authors were taking more pains to get their background facts 'vetted' for them by inside contacts; and frequently now the investigator was a professional C.I.D. inspector like Ngaio Marsh's Roderick Alleyn or Michael Innes's John Appleby. There were more verses in *Punch*:

> 'It must be a plausible method of killing
>   And solved in the end by an obvious clue;
> I don't like a crime, be it never so thrilling,
>   Unless I can feel that it *might* have been true.'

Then there were the Filmland policemen. Mack Sennett had started the Keystone Cops in 1912; but they were still popular in the 'twenties. There was an article in *Punch* about them.

'A POSSE OF STALWART POLICEMEN HAS LEAPED INTO A CAR AND IS HURTLING TO YOUR ASSISTANCE.'

[*Punch*, Jan. 21, 1925

'If he occasionally appears inefficient in the controlling of traffic that is travelling in various directions at an average speed of seventy miles an hour, his promptness and industry in other branches of constabulary duty evoke admiration. You cannot break a window or assault a fellow-citizen in Filmland without having at least a dozen constables on your track before you have reached the end of the street. If you are in trouble and ring up a police-station, the inspector in charge does not waste time asking for trivial details. Long before you have finished working your mouth, he has slammed down the receiver and a posse of stalwart policemen has leaped into a car and is hurtling to your assistance. The Filmland criminal is the most harassed person on earth.'

When the talking pictures arrived, *Punch* called them 'the shouties' or 'the squeakies'. There were cartoons of Jack Hulbert as a policeman in the film *Jack's the Boy** and another of George Robey in a London Hippodrome revue.

J·H·DOWD·

THE NEW BLUE BOY
Jack . . . . . JACK HULBERT
[*Punch*, July 13, 1932

GEORGE ROBEY
IN 'BITS AND PIECES'
[*Punch*, Jan. 4, 1928

* Jack Hulbert was to do yeoman service in the Metropolitan Special Constabulary, which he joined in 1940, rising to the rank of Commandant at Headquarters, where he had particular responsibility for the recruitment of women Specials.

14

The 'twenties saw the rise and spread of night clubs. There were respectable supper
clubs where the law was observed and cabaret shows of artistic merit were put on.
(The dubious attractions of 'strip tease' had not yet been accepted as tolerable by the
general public.) Infringements of the liquor licensing laws—whether by overstepping
the hours or by the device of 'bottle parties'—were the fly in the ointment, and in
view of the difficulties in enforcing the law, policemen in plain clothes had to be sent
in as ordinary members to get evidence of illegalities before clubs could be raided.
Punch commented more than once on the expenses incurred by them on champagne

'I TELL YOU THEY *ARE* POLICE OFFICERS. THEY'RE DRINKING CHAMPAGNE.'

[*Punch*, Oct. 19, 1932

bought and fees to dance hostesses. E. V. Knox in one article says: 'The police constable's dancing was superb; in tying a white tie he had no equal amongst the constabulary in the land.' A. P. Herbert, who felt strongly about *agents provocateurs*, in an article called 'The New Sleuths' in his series 'The Man About Town', said in 1924:

> 'This is an age of State action, in crime as in other things. Few of the minor crimes are now committed without the assistance of the police. Most crimes could be taken out of the hands of a crowd of bungling amateurs and given over to a few trained and trustworthy policemen.'

A year or two later *Punch*'s Summer Number contained a cartoon entitled 'The Cop and the Vamp—A Night Club Idyll' starring Joynson Hicks as a P.C. waggling an admonitory finger at a dancer.*

'I WON'T BE HOME TO-NIGHT, MUMS, BUT EVERYTHING'S *quite* ALL RIGHT—I'VE BEEN ARRESTED.'
[*Punch*, Feb. 12, 1936]

It was in 1928 that the most notorious club, 'The 43', was raided by Sergeant Goddard, when Mrs. Meyrick and everyone there were taken to Vine Street. Mrs Meyrick went to prison, but the club was not finally closed until 1932.

* It was about this time that the late Hannen Swaffer published his *Who's Who* which contained an article about 'Jix' in which he claims:

> 'When I sent him the facts about the night club scandal, and its pollution of the police, he immediately touched a bell and said: "Send for the Commissioner." He came straight over from Scotland Yard. "Close all the night clubs immediately," said the Home Secretary.'

Perhaps, if Jix listened so closely to him, it was because, he tells us, the Home Office were confused as to his identity and addressed more than one letter to him as 'The Reverend Canon Swaffer'.

In his 'Misleading Cases', under the heading 'The Spy System', in the case of *R. v. The Commissioner of Police, a Chief Inspector, an Inspector, a Sergeant and Constable Boot*, accused 'at the instance of a public-minded citizen Mr Albert Haddock' of conspiracy to do certain unlawful acts, A. P. Herbert makes Mr Justice Swallow say, in his address to the jury:

> 'By the wise ordinances of our land it is unlawful to buy or sell chocolates after half-past nine in the evening, or to buy cigarettes, cigars or matches after 8. These regulations are in line with the ancient tradition of this island, which has always been to discourage and irritate the foreign visitor by every form of inconvenience and restriction, and so dispose him to return to his own country.
>
> At the hour of 8.5 p.m. the defendant Boot, being in plain clothes, asked the barmaid for a packet of cigarettes. She refused but he pleaded with her, and she at last relented. Boot then took her name and address and informed her that a charge would be made.
>
> The "*agent provocateur*" is a French expression; there is no other phrase, and for a very good reason: the idea is so repugnant to British notions of fair play and decency that it has never found expression in our language. It is not employed for the suppression of the major crimes; no constable causes himself to be murdered or robbed for the protection of the public; but it is the constant support of small prosecutions for small offences wisely invented by righteous people for the prevention or hindrance of public enjoyment . . .
>
> If you return a verdict of Not Guilty, I shall ignore your verdict.'

Sir William Joynson-Hicks, familiarly known as 'Jix' (later Lord Brentford), had become Home Secretary in 1924 and held the office for five years. He was a Solicitor, who had been in Parliament since 1908, when he had defeated Winston Churchill at Manchester. (He was for fifteen years Chairman of the Automobile Association, and the first Chairman of the Safety First Association.) But *Punch* was often critical of his manner.

> 'There is a carefree clumsiness about the Home Secretary on the floor of the House that excites suspicion where no suspicion is called for', said 'Toby M.P.' 'He will make a simple announcement in a way that suggests that he is hiding something up his sleeve which he will produce later with dramatic effect.'

A. P. Herbert had a particular down on him.

> 'For this is law, I wish to say
> While office I enjoy, Sir:
> Whatever other parts I play
> I'll be the Principal Boy, Sir.'

he wrote, to the air of 'The Vicar of Bray', in one of his 'Ballads for Broadbrows'. In another, on a report that 'the Home Secretary has announced that he may soon have to deal with Books, as he has dealt with the Parks', each verse ended: 'Will no one muzzle Auntie Jix?'

It was in 1928 that A. P. Herbert, not yet an M.P. himself, put Topsy into Parliament so that her letters to her bosom friend Trix might cover a wider field. Her letters included the following:

'I've taken to *tormenting* the man Hicks with *Parliamentary* questions, my dear he's like a *baby* the *moment* you leave him alone he does something *too* ghastly . . . suddenly he erupted with three perfectly *flatulent* speeches about DORA being *dead*, and of course the very same day I saw a man was fined because the number-plates on his car were too *large*, and also a *stainless* publican was prosecuted *merely* darling because somebody played the piano in the *bar* and the criminals present joined in the *chorus* and the man hadn't a *music*-licence and of course there were *three* detectives sniffing *busily* at the window, can you *see* the picture, so *English* darling, because my dear it seems if one man sings at the piano it's *too* lawful but if *three* men sing it's felonious, well darling I put down a question . . . and started *pelting* the person with *Supplementaries*, and I said Well if *that's* the law had he taken *any* steps to have it altered during the last *four years*, and he took six words to say *No* as the *verbose* custom is, so I said *Is* it not a fact that the *sole offence* in this case was that people were *enjoying themselves* and did he *still* think DORA was *dead* . . . my dear his *one* idea is raids and regulations, my dear *here* he is in 1929 still *loudly* announcing that he is *definitely* going to utterly *clean-up* the night-life of London, and the *sole* fruit and blossom of four years' *hysterical* cleaning is that the *police* are in a *septic* mess, my dear it's *rather* hilarious when you come to think of it, *half* Scotland Yard quite *swearing* before the Police Commission that the police are *too* impeccable and the other half *nose-deep* in the *most* insanitary police scandals.

Anyhow my *next* question was *Has* Hicks done *anything* during the last four years and does he *propose* to do anything to reform and codify the *diseased* Betting Laws, well my dear he *bleated* in the negative as usual . . . so the next day I did the same about the *Divorce* Laws and the Licensing Laws . . . my dear he's one protracted NO, *too* marvellous at stamping the heavy foot, but *where* is the helping hand? My dear his *one* idea is raids and regulations.'

A full-page cartoon in 1928 by Bernard Partridge, entitled 'Jix Unlimited', shows the Home Secretary at his desk blandly contemplating documents inscribed 'A Caution to Coppers', and 'My New Prayer Book by Jix', while strewed about the floor round his feet are other folios inscribed 'A New Guide to Night Clubs'; 'Taxis for Two'; 'Red Gold or the Moscow Menace'; 'Greater Brighton', and 'My Past, or the Dog who Took the Right Turning'. (Home Office archives would no doubt tell us what particular incidents the last two referred to.) Another full-page cartoon showed him, dressed as a beadle with a bell, being told by Mr Punch: 'Stop your tinkling, Jicks.'

'Toby M.P.' reports that the Home Secretary made a brief but lucid defence of the ukase which forbids a policeman to chew gum while on duty: there was a grave risk, he explained, that the officer might blow the chewing-gum into his whistle, and so be unable to function with that instrument.

Towards the end of 1927, there was a brief paragraph in 'Charivaria':

'It is rumoured that, following recent police disclosures, the Home Secretary is to hold an enquiry into the law of the Meads and Persians.'

THE LIBERTY OF THE SUBJECT

The Derby Dog. 'I ENTIRELY ENDORSE THE RECENT DEMAND FOR AN INQUIRY INTO WHAT I CAN ONLY STIGMATISE AS THE TYRANNICAL METHODS OF THE POLICE FORCE.'

[*Punch,* June 6, 1928

By 1928, the Metropolitan Police were in bad odour with the public.*

ROSES AND EGGS

A mixed reception at the tribunal theatre

[*Punch*, July 18, 1928

* 'In the years 1926–1928', says Sir John Moylan in the 2nd (1934) Edition of his book, *Scotland Yard and the Metropolitan Police*, 'it was found necessary to have several inquests into Metropolitan police matters. An impression got abroad that all these were in the nature of investigations into police misconduct. This was an entirely false view of the facts: they were mostly concerned with questions of policy and procedure, and as to the desirability of altering the law. But underlying them all was perhaps something in the nature of a general questioning of police methods and an idea that the relations of police and public were not as cordial as they used to be.'

There was a Hyde Park case which excited a good deal of surprise and doubts in the House, leading E. V. Knox to write in *Punch*:

> 'O Robert Peel, I wonder how
> You'd contemplate this Savidge row?
> Can you survey without remorse
> These strictures on a splendid force?'

'Jix' was accused of whitewashing the police. There followed the appointment of a Royal Commission on Police Powers and Procedure, which reported in the following

Sir William Joynson-Hicks (in Hyde Park). 'OF COURSE THIS FIGURE DOESN'T REALLY WANT ANYTHING DONE TO IT, BUT A LITTLE DUSTING WON'T DO IT ANY HARM.'
[*Punch*, July 11, 1928

year. There was also a change of Commissioner, and several debates on the new appointment in the Commons, duly reported in *Punch*'s 'Essence of Parliament':

'Mr Snowden intimated that a soldier among policemen is a dreadful thing; he may give them the military mind. Further, that a retired soldier of sixty-five would be able to give them precious little else. Everybody knows that Lord Byng has not got a military mind to pass on, and that his physical and mental vigour are those of a two-year-old. Mr Snowden also thought that the new Commissioner should have been recruited from within the Force. The answer to that was simple—the police are under a cloud of suspicion, merited or otherwise, and with a far-reaching investigation of police methods pending it would be foolish and might be fatal to appoint a top-policeman to a post whose holder *must* enjoy the confidence of the public.*

GLOVES *VERSUS* TRUNCHEON
MR PHILIP SNOWDEN AND SIR WILLIAM JOYNSON-HICKS.
[*Punch*, July 18, 1928

Unfortunately the Home Secretary was rather stopped from making that reply by the persistence with which he has contended that there is really nothing wrong. He did admit that the situation called for a Commissioner of very exceptional abilities, but qualified it by saying that what was wanted was not a "reorganisation" of the Force but "reinspiration". And he added the perfectly futile suggestion that the "sub-acid" feeling against the police was probably due to the coming of the motor-car.

Mr Saklatvala's declaration that the police are the brutal minions of the capitalist in the warfare of class failed to rouse the answering cheer.'

* A quarter of a century was to pass before a man who had joined the police service as a constable and worked his way up to the very top was to become Commissioner of Police of the Metropolis.

Field Marshal Lord Byng of Vimy had been looking forward to well-earned leisure in retirement, after capturing the heart of Canada as Governor-General; but 'Jix' persuaded him to accept the post as 'a stern call to duty'. 'I am the most readily sackable person in the world,' he said, when the Labour party came into office, 'so please don't hesitate.' But it was three years before the government would accept his resignation; and under his 'benign influence' the force was to recover confidence in itself, and the public's confidence in the police was restored.

P.C. BYNG COMES ON HIS BEAT

Mrs Britannia. 'HE'S ALL RIGHT. I LIKED HIM IN KHAKI AND I LIKE HIM IN BLUE.'

[Lord Byng of Vimy is about to take up his duties as Chief Commissioner of Police.]

[*Punch*, Oct. 31, 1928

He is (I think) the only Commissioner of Police whom *Punch* honoured with a full-page portrait cartoon in the last seventy years. When he retired, C. L. Graves wrote:

'None of the laurels that you won and wore
For splendid services in Peace and War
Proved in the winning of them quite as hard
As those which crown you when you leave "The Yard"—
—Your irksome duties resolutely done—
Once more the finest Force under the sun,
Regenerated by your selfless zeal,
And the best bulwark of the common weal.'

During his Commissionership, the Metropolitan Police celebrated their centenary, with an inspection by the Prince of Wales in Hyde Park, and a march past Buckingham Palace. *Punch* marked the centenary with Raven Hill's full-page drawing, 'Robert our Friend and Guardian', which is reproduced in the introductory chapter of this book.

1930 was the year in which the United States went 'wet' again. E. V. Knox had some lengthy verses, 'The Broken Bootlegger's Lament', from which it is only possible to quote one stanza (somehow reminiscent of Kipling's '*The Mary Gloster*').

'The old dry days are over, the best that we ever had,
And the people can get their highballs without the help of your dad,
The squads of tame policemen who came each morn for their graft,
And the yacht that once we cruised on, with the two quick-firers aft.'

At home it was the year of mixed bathing at Lansbury's Lido; and the word 'hiking' had come into use for organised country walks in herds. *Punch* had a full-page drawing of a country policeman regulating four streams of hikers converging in the wide open spaces.

1932 was the year in which the telephone number of Scotland Yard was changed to Whitehall 1212, and *Punch* had some verses 'after Lewis Carroll' called 'Beaverbrocky':

' 'Twas grilling, and the sleuthy coves
      Did gird and grumble on parade;
Official flimsies came in droves
      And the home truths dismayed.

Beware the jabbering, my son,
      The pars that bite, the pens that mock!
Beware the gupgup herd who're run
      By fulminous Beaverbrook!

He'll take his verbal sword in hand;
　　Long time your ranks to mow he sought;
He'll phone (you'll see) the C.I.D.
　　Re murderers (uncaught).

One two! One two! Whitehall (you're through)
　　etc. etc. etc.

The 'Information Room' had been started in Lord Byng's time, though the '999' dialling system was not to be arranged with the G.P.O. until 1937. This is *not* automatically a police call—it is an emergency call, on receipt of which the Exchange will ask whether you want police, fire or ambulance service. The cartoon shows someone whose call produced one of each.

'. . . I SIMPLY DIALLED "999".'
[*Punch*, Jan. 26, 1938

'. . . AND REMEMBER, DEAR, FOR CASES OF EMERGENCY THE NUMBER IS 999.'
[*Punch*, March 29, 1939

The period of unemployment was at its height—which made police recruiting easier —though police had to share in the general economy pay cuts; but there were unemployed disturbances, of which Sir John Gilmour, Home Secretary later in the year, is reported by *Punch* as having told the House:

'He had proof that Moscow money and Communist organisation were behind these demonstrations, and stoutly defended the patience and long-suffering moderation of the police. The disorder was premeditated, as was proved by the significant fact that after the affray 37 police officers and only 13 civilians were treated for injuries.'

After the calm, the hurricane. Lord Byng was succeeded in 1931 by Lord Trenchard. ('Father' of the Royal Air Force). He found Scotland Yard due for a spring-cleaning— as Henderson had found it in 1869, and Macready in 1918; but he had taken the post on the understanding that he would not stay more than three years. In fact he remained another year—long enough to lead the Jubilee parade of police of all forces in Hyde Park in 1935 (the centenary of the Municipal Corporations Act of 1835). During those four years he tore up practically everything by the roots, but left some things not firmly replanted.

The Commissioner's Annual Report, which is laid before Parliament and circulated to the press, had tended to become colourless and largely statistical. Lord Trenchard saw that it gave a real opportunity for explanation and propaganda; and in the Report for his first full year of office, he had set out the general principles on which he saw need for changes.

Punch in 'Essence of Parliament' reported Sir Herbert Samuel, then Home Secretary, as paying tribute to Lord Trenchard for enforcing the principle of promotion by merit, not by mere seniority.

The Metropolitan Police Bill, introduced in May 1933, was hotly debated on several days in both Houses of Parliament, being bitterly contested by Labour members. 'Toby M.P.' reported:

> 'It might have fared a good deal worse than it did at the point of Mr Lansbury's laborious and class-conscious sallies. The opposition were not particular, however. They wanted to hear the Bill denounced as a class measure, an attempt to "militarise" the police by an imported Airman who knew nothing about police work, and a bright scheme for getting more jobs for the unemployed sons of the "officer class".

'NOW THEN, BOY! YOU MUSTN'T STAND IN PEOPLE'S WAY. YOU MUST MOVE ON!'
[*After a Cartoon of Sir Robert Peel, by John Leech, 'Punch,'* April 11, 1846.]
Mr Lansbury and Sir John Gilmour
[*Punch,* May 31, 1933

The Bill may be assailed more vigorously still in Committee on the ground that its intentions are excellent, but its provisions—notably that providing for short-term service and the introduction of the "college policeman" into the higher ranks —will not in fact achieve the objects sought to be attained.'*

Five weeks later,

'The Metropolitan Police Bill has emerged practically unscathed from the Standing Committee. . . . Mr Lunn, who led the assault today, accused the Government of "establishing a body of snobs within the Force". Mr Cocks talked about "the new Hitler force which the Government are setting up to shoot down the workers of the country". Sir John Gilmour's reply contained the frank admission that they were now drawing "somewhere else" the line which had always been drawn between certain police officers of high rank and the Police Federation. . . . The short-term men would give better service than the eight thousand now in the Force who had reached an age when there was no hope of further promotion.

"Where on earth are you ever going to find a Force in which everyone expects promotion?" demanded the Member for Limehouse (Mr Attlee).'

The third reading was carried by 210 votes to 52.

There were many jokes at that time about the better educated policeman. Ronald Frankau wrote and sang in the theatre:

'We'll be reading police-craft at Oxford,
    And attending the new Rozzer-course.
Our knowledge of classics will be quite unique,
    And to prove to the crooks all the lingos we speak,
We'll warn 'em in Latin and charge 'em in Greek,
    When you've fellows like me in the Force.'†

There was a whole page of drawings in *Punch* of a young recruit sitting down to try to cope with 'The Examination Questions for our Well Educated Young Policemen'. He has no difficulty with such questions as 'Trace the causes of the place of execution being moved from Tyburn to odd spots' or 'Describe in detail how you would proceed by the use of simple apparatus to find the density of the hot air in the House of Commons'; but when he comes to 'State what influence on crime Bill Sikes would have had if he had been a Senior Wrangler', he throws in his hand.

---

* In this Mr Punch was in the long run proved to be prophetic. Lord Trenchard's scheme for the recruitment of a proportion of the force on short-term engagements was based on an innovation which he had introduced into the Royal Air Force. It was part of his plan to have a younger force, so improving the career prospects of the long-service policeman. The results were disappointing; the scheme produced strong reactions among the police, and was discontinued before the war by his successor.

The Hendon College was closed down on the outbreak of war. After the war, a National Police College was opened elsewhere. This will be referred to when we come to that period.

† Published by the Peter Maurice Music Co. Ltd.

THE POLISHED FORCE

[The Second Annual Report made by Lord Trenchard recommends the raising of
the 'educational level' of the Metropolitan Police.]

[*Punch*, May 10, 1933

It was in 1934 that the Prince of Wales formally opened Lord Trenchard's Police College, in the buildings originally put up by Graham White for a Country Club at London Aerodrome at Hendon, but since converted into a factory. The idea of a College for higher training of police was not new. In 1930 a Committee appointed by Mr Clynes, then Home Secretary in a Labour Government, had sketched out a scheme for a national police college, which had inspired E. V. Knox to some verses in *Punch*:

> 'There shall our boys, for evermore
>   Matriculating, seek their solace
> Under the great Vice-Chancellor,
>   The very learned Edgar Wallace.
>
> Here on the thrice-enchanted ground,
>   Conversant with Gaboriau's hints,
> Shall pious benefactors found
>   A Faculty of Finger-Prints.'

That Committee's report had been shelved for various reasons—principally the current economy crisis. Lord Trenchard was not prepared to wait for agreement to be obtained from all the provincial Chief Constables and Police Authorities, so the Hendon College scheme related solely to the London Metropolitan police. An idea got round that the Hendon Police College was exclusively for direct entrants from the public schools and universities, who would come straight in with silver spoons in their mouths,

SLEUTHS: THE OLD SCHOOL TIE AND THE OLD SCHOOL

Sergt. Oliver . . . . Mr Richard Murdoch
Inspector Giffnock . . . . . . Mr Syd Walker

[*Punch*, Oct. 28, 1936

and a short cut to all the higher ranks. In actual fact, nearly three quarters of the two hundred men who passed through that police college in the five years of its existence had already been serving as constables before they were picked out for higher training. But 'The Old School Tie' was the current music-hall joke of the Western Brothers. *Punch* had a cartoon of Richard Murdoch as a public school policeman in a musical comedy at the Saville Theatre. A humorous drawing showed a householder saying of the burglar just arrested:

'The distressing part of it is, Officer, the fellow is apparently an old Cuthbertonian—my dear old school,'

to which the New Policeman replies:

'Yes, I know—most painful; mine too!'

The drawing reproduced here shows the constable coming on the burglar at work and falling back reluctantly on time-honoured police parlance.

'AND WHAT, IF YOU'LL PARDON THE CLICHÉ, IS ALL THIS 'ERE?'
[*Punch*, Nov. 23, 1938

There was something of a crime wave in the early 'thirties, with epidemics of bag-snatching and smash-and-grab raids, and house-breaking by the 'cat burglar'. (When Peel had been launching his New Police, a hundred years before, he had spoken in the House of Commons of 'the increasing mechanical ingenuity of the age'. Then, of course, he had in mind the new railways, which would make the criminal more mobile: now criminals had begun to use motor-cars, and the motor bandit was the modern equiva-lent of the highwayman.)

15

'So far', said a paragraph in 'Charivaria', 'the police have been unable to capture "Flannel-Foot", the most silent and elusive of London burglars. But no doubt they will, just as soon as he tries to park his car in some unauthorised place.'*

'WELL, CLEVER! HAVING MADE OUR ESCAPE TO THE ROOF, WHAT DO WE DO NEXT?'

[*Punch*, July 18, 1934

A. P. Herbert had learned with surprise that the policeman was allowed to leave his beat for half-an-hour's meal break.

'Now, Sir,' he wrote to Mr Punch, 'when the enterprising burglar's not a-burgling, it is our pleasure to think that the constable is a-basking with a bun. But it is of the essence of a tea-interval (as of an armistice) that both sides agree to suspend operations at the same time; and the question is, can we rely on our burglars to observe this elementary understanding?'

Commenting on an article in the press shortly afterwards that there had been a

* 'Flannelfoot' was finally run to earth, after operating successfully for nearly four years, by means of records on a special map on which the places where he abandoned the bicycles which he stole for his jobs were linked.

fundamental change in the police beat system, there were some verses headed 'The Hard Hit Burglar':

'Although conveyances more fleet
     Are handier for shock work,
The Force till lately used its feet,
And every copper tramped a beat
     As regular as clockwork.

For years their loyalty to hikes
     By schedule was tremendous;
But nowadays the dirty tikes
Resort to push- and motor-bikes
     And cars to apprehend us.'

It was also in the early 'thirties that A. P. Herbert was accentuating his drive for the Liberty of the Subject. Satirically anticipating by ten years what the Report of the Licensing Committee might be, he made them recommend uniform hours for the consumption of alcohol for licensed premises, clubs and private houses, the police to have the same unconditional right of entry into each.

'The police authorities point out that most murders take place in private houses, and that they were hampered by the antiquated regulations which forbade them to enter a private house without a search warrant', he wrote. 'Until they had the same right of entry to a private house as they had to a public-house, they could not guarantee that there would be no more murders. . . . The possibility of a sudden visit from the police at any hour of the twenty-four must have a beneficial influence on the home in many ways, over and above the mere enforcement of the licensing laws . . . There seems to have grown up a popular impression that a man in his own home is entitled to do what he likes. Witnesses representing various public bodies had been heard; the private citizen was not represented, since it would be pointed out that as all the witnesses had homes of their own, they might be assumed to express the opinion of the average citizen. One hostile witness had gone so far as to quote "An Englishman's home is his castle": it would be more in tune with the ideals and practices of the present time to say "An Englishman's home is his police-station".'

In the Misleading Case of *R.* v. *Boot and Others* in 1933, Constable Boot is charged, with two burglars, with being an *agent provocateur*. Counsel defending the burglars says:

'In the old days we trusted the people to look after themselves; but now . . . we can't trust them to do more than a few of the things we tell them to; and so we have inspectors and spies to prevent the people from doing what we tell them not to. . . . Many potential wrong-doers have a tiresome habit of loitering about and refusing to do the wrong thing which the spy is there to prevent them from doing. Therefore the most economical method has been found to be for the spy to arrange for the wrong-doer to do wrong on a date when it is convenient for the spy to be there.'

(In this case the two burglars got stiff sentences, but Mr Justice Wool reluctantly tells the jury to acquit Constable Boot.)

In 1930 Raven Hill had a full-page cartoon showing a uniformed 'P.C. Clynes' (then Home Secretary in the Labour Government) stopping John Bull from taking a ticket in a hospital sweepstake.

> 'Now then, what's this?' he says. 'Gambling for a good cause! Nobody in this country is allowed to gamble, except with bookies or on the tote.'

In 1933, while the Betting and Lotteries Act of 1934 was on the stocks, the Court of Criminal Appeal—in another of A.P.H.'s Misleading Cases—quashes the conviction of a publican who had been induced, after refusing several times, to sell a ticket for the Irish Sweepstake to a policewoman in disguise; and the Lord Chief Justice says:

> 'I cannot in this Court form phrases which would sufficiently express my disgust at these manœuvres. The "Third Degree" means little more than continual badgering; and in this case he was continually badgered, not to confess, but to commit the offence. . . . The offence, if any, was the policewoman's, and I order that she be arrested and charged.'

Two years later, it is Albert Haddock himself who is charged at Bow Street with an offence under the new Act—he having attempted ingeniously to evade the prohibition of sending tickets for the Irish Hospitals Sweepstake Fund through the post by sending a carrier-pigeon to bring it back to him from Dublin. He is charged with 'distributing' the ticket through the pigeon to a constable who had picked it up and confiscated it. The Chief Magistrate says:

> 'However deeply the Court may detest the low ethical standards of Mr Haddock, as exemplified, first, in his evident eagerness to acquire thirty thousand pounds otherwise than by honest toil, and, secondly, in his willingness to degrade a dumb and defenceless bird into the base service of a lottery—I must order that the bird and the defendant be re-united. Costs against the Police.'

A year later still, 'Toby M.P.' could report that an anti-Pool Betting Bill 'was happily flung out with no mean force', Mr A. P. Herbert (now an M.P.) having 'begged the puritans for God's sake to leave a little folly in the world'.

Punch was maintaining its somewhat cynical attitude to the allowances being made for 'delinquents' on the evidence of psychologists. In 1929, quoting from a newspaper case in which a neurotic young thief had been saved from a whipping by the plea of a doctor that he was 'too introspective' for such a punishment to be safe, there had been some verses:

'Burkanhare will now appeal; it surely cannot be
That *all* our Judges set at naught the higher psychology;
And the point his counsel's going to make, as strongly as he can
Is that hanging might prove fatal to an introspective man.'

In 1931, when a magistrate, sentencing an offender for stealing money, dealt severely with the plea that he had a 'mental kink', there were some verses, headed 'Rough Justice':

'Unversed in the abundant store
Of modern psychologic lore
Our callous narrow-minded beaks
Have little sympathy with freaks;

Oh bright young persons, on the brink
Of any high uproarious jink,
Pause for a moment—pause and think;
It will not keep you out of clink
To plead you have a mental kink.'

And in 1936, on the theme that many offences are stated to be due to a phobia or fear of those in authority, there were more verses:

'When in my pleasing childhood's sports
    I tore my books and inked my collar,
And by my terminal reports
    Caused my Papa a deal of dolour,
He would not have been nearly so annoyed
Had he perused the works of Jung and Freud.

And when we feel the call of crime,
    The lure of champerty or arson
(Or still more heinous Cockney rhyme,)
    'Tis nice to know the guilt will fasten
On editors, police, and such-like pests
Who rouse these terrors in our blameless breasts.'

The abolition of any general speed limit by the Road Traffic Act of 1930 resulted in the end of speed traps, for the most part; but as Parliament had been promised that the police would concentrate on dangerous or careless driving, many more constables had to be taken off beats for fixed point traffic duties. Police motor patrols equipped with loud-speakers, a recent innovation, now came into full use; and young policemen who had hitherto driven their own motor-cycles on their off days, with wife or girl-friend in the side-car, now sometimes found themselves forgetting, with their eyes on the road, who their passenger was.

Absent-minded young Policeman (newly transferred to the mobile squad). 'WARM ENOUGH, DARLING?'
[*Punch*, April 12, 1933

Their instructions were 'to give suitable advice in a pleasant and courteous manner', and they earned the nick-name of 'Courtesy Cops'. In trivial cases they were authorised to give verbal warnings on the spot, the primary purpose being the prevention of accidents rather than a lot of proceedings to enforce the strict letter of the law; but some motorists, women in particular, were apt to expect unlimited latitude.

'Now-now-now,' one 'Fair Motorist' is pictured in *Punch* saying, 'put that notebook away. A few gentle words of warning are all we need,' while another asks the village P.C. taking notes: 'Wouldn't you like us to have this as a naughty little secret between us?' And there is the drawing of the young couple in the sports car, stopping to look back to see who it is they have knocked off his motor-cycle into the ditch, and one of them says with relief: 'Thank goodness it's only a courtesy cop.' But even the worm will turn; and there is a picture by Charles Grave of the bucolic village policeman, on his back in the ditch, saying to the driver who has stopped and got out of his car: 'You an' me's goin' to have three minutes' private talk, an' then I'll produce my notebook an' be official.'

THE LATEST COLOSSUS OF ROADS

Policeman (in the manner of Shakespeare). 'THERE IS NOTHING EITHER DANGEROUS OR SAFE BUT MY THINKING MAKES IT SO.'

[By the new Traffic Act the speed-limit is abolished and it devolves upon the police to decide what constitutes dangerous driving.]

[*Punch*, Aug. 13, 1930

Punch had one rather unkind full-page cartoon by Bernard Partridge which seemed to suggest that the pedestrian had now acquired the double-risk of exposure to the 'speed cop' as well as the 'speed-hog'; but there was another cartoon, showing Herbert

THE LAW'S ACCELERATIONS

First Pedestrian. 'How did you get laid out?'
Second Pedestrian. 'Speed-hog. And you?'
First Pedestrian. 'Speed-cop.'

[To carry out the new Traffic Act, a thousand mobile police are to be mounted on motor-cycles, with the idea of pursuing and overtaking those who drive to the public danger.]

[*Punch,* Dec. 10, 1930

Morrison (then Minister of Transport) promising 'P.C. Clynes' the complete elimination of the road-hog. Soon 'Toby M.P.' could report the Home Secretary explaining in the House of Commons:

'The unwittingly offending motorist is to be kindly cautioned instead of being soaked with a summons, while the really dangerous driver will get it even more effectively in the neck, all to the greater saving of time and trouble for police, magistrates and public alike.'

GRAND TRANSFORMATION; OR, THE DISAPPEARING ROAD-HOG

Harlequin . . . . Mr Morrison.
Policeman . . . . Mr Clynes.

[*Punch*, Dec. 24, 1930

There was a 'Safety Week', which prompted Owen Seaman to some verses:

'Six days of respite! Such a debt
I should indeed be more than sorry
Not to repay in kind, and thus
I've sworn I will not kill a bus
By stamping on it, or upset
        A courteous lorry.'

while Raven Hill did a full-page cartoon, 'The Road Beautiful', in which motorist and pedestrian are shown, each waiting, bowing to the other and saying in unison: 'After you, Sir!' But there had also been a drawing of the flapper, warned that she is going to be charged with driving to the public danger, protesting: 'Dash it, Constable, is that fair? It isn't Safety Week yet.' Some of them seem to have been incapable of taking in any Highway Code. 'Didn't you see the caution sign?' the village P.C. asks the lady driver, only to get the reply: 'Gosh! Is that what it was? I thought it was something to do with the Y.M.C.A.'

Young Lady-Motorist (*in conflict with the law*). 'IF IT WASN'T SO ABSURDLY IMPOSSIBLE, I'D SAY YOU WERE TOO BIG FOR YOUR BOOTS.'

[*Punch*, June 1, 1932

The launching of a Thames Taxi Service in 1932—based on Chelsea, plying between Putney and Greenwich—prompted A. P. Herbert to renew his efforts to get a water-bus service revived by the L.C.C., as some contribution to the problem of traffic congestion in the London streets. (In the old days, it could be claimed that the Thames, besides being the quickest and most pleasant, was the safest from footpads and highwaymen. Now the public made little use of the Thames, except on the pleasure steamers and a few open launches making short excursions from Westminster Pier down to Greenwich or round the docks.)

In an open letter in *Punch* to Mr Pybus (then Minister of Transport) A.P.H. urged him to leave behind him a fleet of 'Pybuses' plying up and down the Thames.

'London's river, the largest and longest highway in the town, a highway requiring neither upkeep nor repair, is an empty and an almost useless obstacle, carrying none of the people from their homes to their offices. . . . The "Pybus"—not the old, slow, unpunctual, smelly paddle-steamers, but a modern all-weather motor-vessel carrying 2–300 passengers—could do fifteen miles an hour (with the tide) through parts of London where the tram or motor-bus can scarcely do five.'

(But it was not until the Festival of Britain year that a Water-bus service operated on a small scale to Battersea.)

A. P. Herbert was turning a good deal of his attention to the right to existence of the pedestrian. He had already, in the case of *Haddock* v. *Thwale* in the Court of Appeal, let Albert Haddock—whose action for damages against a motorist who had knocked him down had been dismissed by the L.C.J.—claim (relying on the leading case of *Rylands* v. *Fletcher*):

'Thwale's motor-car should in law be regarded as a wild beast; and the boast of its makers that it contains the concentrated power of forty-five horses makes the comparison just. If a man were to bring upon the public street forty-five horses tethered together and were to gallop them at their full speed past a frequented cross-roads, no lack of agility, judgment or presence of mind in the pedestrian would be counted such negligence as to excuse his injury. The Master of the Rolls, giving judgement, said that they held the owner of the motor-car to be liable for the consequences of releasing a dangerous and uncontrollable monster, and awarded heavy damages. The Court also ordered the motor-car to be destroyed.'

'Reduce speed and you reduce death', he contends in an article in the form of a letter to the Editor of *Punch*, on the outbreak of manslaughter on the roads of our country.

'I do not refer to the comparatively trivial activities of bandits and gunmen, but to the destruction of peaceful citizens using the king's highway, in motors, on bicycles or a-foot. . . . The speed of motor-cars is two parts impatience begot of unpunctuality, one part rudeness and one part necessity. When I am Dictator of the Roads, I shall begin by killing the idea that great speed is important, necessary, or a cause for pride. It may mean a strict execution of the law of homicide, which is that
"*if a man do a thing deliberately which is calculated to endanger the life of another, and it causes his death, he will be guilty of homicide*".'

'What was the cause of the accident?' an old lady is pictured asking an errand boy, to which he replies succinctly: 'Two motorists after the same pedestrian.' And 'Toby M.P.' reports the Home Secretary, asked in the House what would be the position of a pedestrian who attempts to cross the road when the light changes from green to amber, replying that his position would probably be a recumbent one.

'The idea that there is some virtue in the sounding of motor horns as a prelude to a collision', A.P.H. makes Mr Justice Wool say in one of his Misleading Cases, 'has in the past, I am aware, received the thoughtless blessing of magistrates and policemen.

What the defendants say in effect is: "I am a public danger; but once I have shouted 'Look out!—I am coming!' I am not to be blamed for what happens." It is the duty of the defendant's driver so to direct his dangerous vehicle that no warning of his approach is necessary.'

FITTER PEDESTRIANS

Why not organise sprinting races between non-motorists to make
the most of gaps in the traffic?

[*Punch*, June 4, 1930

Motoring casualties had increased considerably since the removal of the speed limit in 1930, heavy vehicles being particular offenders in the matter of excessive speeds. The new by-passes and ribbon development had made fresh death-traps for children, and Bernard Partridge had a grim cartoon showing Mr Punch protesting to the Spirit of 'Progress'. The result was another Road Traffic Act in 1934, imposing the 30-mile speed limit in 'built-up areas'. 'This is a built-up area, Madam,' a George Belcher constable is pictured saying to a lady driver, 'and you've been goin' more than thirty miles an hour,' to which she replies: 'Don't be silly. I haven't been out an hour yet!'

Police cars were now equipped with gongs, and *Punch* had various pictures of people taking alarm at the fire engine bell or even the muffin man's bell, while a cabin

passenger on a liner is shown complaining that the dinner gong rung by a steward reminds him too much of the police gong.

A suggestion that a mobile section of the women police should be formed—there was
indeed a music-hall song of the period, 'Gertie, the Girl with the Gong'—inspired more
than one picture-joke bringing in a policewoman on a motor-bicycle.

WILL THIS

BE CHASED BY THIS?

[*Punch*, Feb. 25, 1931

There was more than one cartoon of Hore-Belisha, Minister of Transport from 1934 to 1937, who gave his name to the Belisha Beacons set up to mark pedestrian crossings—later to be described by A.P.H.'s 'Topsy', in one of her later letters to her bosom friend:

> 'My dear you remember or don't you the Belisha Beacons, which however mocked were a *meritorious* notion and the one thing that gives a pedestrian any *hope* of a future, because as long as he gives reasonable notice it's *not* the done thing to mow him down between the studs, in fact the motors are supposed to *slow* and let him over. . . . It does *not* signify if the orange blob is absent through blitzing because they made a *special* law in the war, but my dear as Haddock says does a *single* driver know all this, or if he does could he *conceivably* care *less, too* often he says when making a stately passage through the studs he's merely *blown* off by the rudest hoots and has to leap a cubit or two to escape some *rocketing* vehicle.'

Mr Punch, commenting in 'Charivaria' on the regular big annual increase in the numbers of cars on the roads, says: 'The decrease in pedestrians is not yet available.'

Hire purchase—hitherto met with principally in the sales of sewing machines, pianos and furniture—was now being adopted in car purchase; and there is a picture of a motorist, asked by a constable 'Is that your car, Sir?' answering 'Not until next April.'

Fougasse had a drawing in which the Learner-driver's licence, introduced in the 'thirties, figures. The motorist who has broken down a fence and run his car into a house, protests to the constable who is taking down his particulars: 'But, my dear good man, if one had to pay for all the damage one did, what would be the point of putting "L" on one's car?'

A motor driving school was opened at Hendon, where the late Sir Malcolm Campbell was invited to advise and to test police drivers, and later Lord Cottenham came to organise advanced courses. E. V. Lucas was to write in *Punch*:

> 'I see that 800 policemen are now being trained in order to begin the beneficent work of inculcating good manners among motorists. . . . There was a time when manners were taught in our childhood by parents and schoolmasters. Is it possible that these sources have dried up and that tuition cannot begin until after a car has been acquired? . . . As a start, in addition to the Metropolitan area, they will supervise and, it is to be hoped, correct the manners of Lancashire, Cheshire, Liverpool, Manchester, Salford and Essex. These, we must therefore suppose, are the worst districts; and they must be pretty bad, considering what goes on in Sussex and Surrey.'

Police cars were now equipped with wireless. The police had been using it since the early 'twenties—at first using the dot-and-dash morse code, with aerials of the old 'bedstead' type which could be raised or lowered. Nowadays they have two-way telephony

'Nothing but chamber music, Fred!'
[*Punch*, March 23, 1938

on a special wave-length; but in the intermediate period there were several humorous drawings, playing on the temptation for the policeman to tune in to music or other programmes.

The Metropolitan Police Laboratory was opened at Hendon in 1935. London was not leading the way—indeed some of the continental Police forces had had forensic science laboratories for years. The Metropolitan Police hitherto had called in recognised outside specialists when they had required expert advice or evidence in criminal cases; but in certain parts of the provinces, where outside experts might not be so readily accessible, there had already been developments. Lord Trenchard decided that it was necessary to have a small scientific staff devoting their whole time to such matters. The *Punch* cartoon reproduced here suggests—as the late Sir Arthur Conan Doyle's sons were apt to—that the police would never have thought of it, if Sherlock Holmes had not shown the way, with his microscope and bunsen burner on a small table in a corner of his rooms in Baker Street.

HOLMES, YOU ASTOUND ME!

[The new Metropolitan Police Laboratory for the scientific investigation
of crime was opened at Hendon by the Home Secretary last week.]

[*Punch*, April 17, 1935

Mussolini, Hitler and Franco were occupying principal attention in the pages of
Punch in the early 'thirties—also the financial depression which had followed the great
Wall Street slump. But at home there were the activities of British Fascists. Sir John
Gilmour, the Home Secretary, refused to be panicked by them ('Toby M.P.' was re-
porting in 1934), even by the acquisition of armoured motor-vans by our native Black-
shirts,

> 'which he seemed to think were intended more as a protection against the violent
> egg than as weapons of offence. Black shirts, of course, stain terribly easily.'

There was a full-page cartoon of Sir John Gilmour's nightmare—a parade of
'manikins' in Black, Blue, Green and Brown Shirts; but British Fascism, he told the
House, being safely split into five organisations, as yet called for no restrictions. Sir
Oswald Mosley, he is reported to have told them a few months later, could continue to
change his shirt, but his spots were indelible.

ROBERT THE POOR DEVIL: OR, THE BLUE MAN'S BURDEN
[*Punch*, June 20, 1934

Much work was thrown on the already overburdened police by hunger marches of the unemployed, and Fascist-Communist demonstrations. A.P.H. entered the lists, with an article on the Englishman's right of free speech and public assembly.

'There is nothing about Free Speech in the British Constitution', he wrote. 'There is nothing about it in Magna Carta or the Bill of Rights. It is an entirely modern conception. Our ancestors did not approve of Free Speech; and there is not a great deal of evidence that we do. The citizens who really want to make or listen to speeches are, I believe, a very small fraction of the population. The remarkable thing about these mass demonstrations is always the millions of people who are *not* there. The truth is, I fear, that we are all in favour of free speech as long as we agree with it. This is shown by the increasing use of the word "provocative". If there is to be free speech, it must be free for all; but if that right is going to be exercised in such a manner as to cause a continual public nuisance, the question does arise whether speeches should not be treated in the same manner as beer—that is, licensed, controlled and taxed.

·   ·   ·   ·   ·

I cannot remember that I ever read anything that Sir Oswald Mosley actually said at his numerous meetings. There is always much in the papers about Before and After, but nothing about During.'

In a letter to Mr Punch under the heading 'The Right to Walk', he says:

'*Is there any right of marching in procession through the streets of London?* There is a very good train and bus service in London, and if people want to hold meetings, let them take advantage of these facilities, or walk. But if they walk, let them walk in twos on the pavements as other pedestrians must.'

He goes on to refer to the precedent of American gangsters, who in the end were 'got', not for heroic battles and robberies, but for mean matters of non-payment of income-tax, a Federal offence. 'Free Speech and Assembly sounds good—Obstructing the Traffic does not.'

By 1936 'Toby M.P.' was referring to 'the mutually imbecile clashes between Fascists and Communists' and 'Sir Oswald Mosley's Knuckle-duster Boys obtruding their fancy dress and boorish manners'. There are full-page cartoons by Bernard Partridge of John Bull puzzled or protesting. 'Toby M.P.' talks of 'the attempts of Führer Mosley and his Bashist Boys to turn the East End into a bear garden'; and there was a cartoon of Sir John Simon (now Home Secretary) standing up for the police.

AUNT SALLY SIMON
The Home Secretary stands up for the Police.
[*Punch*, April 1, 1936

Then came the Public Order Bill, 'the natural outcome in a democratic country of Sir Oswald Mosley's haberdashery tactics. . . . The immediate problem for all B.F.s after the passing of the Bill will be the most profitable disposal of their shirts.' There was a cartoon of Mosley visiting the pawnbrokers, and another of Sir John Simon, behind the counter in a gentlemen's outfitters, saying: 'Sorry, Sir, we're not stocking blacks or reds any more, but we can show you some very attractive lines in brown or blue'—the 'Defence Suit'—army, navy or R.A.F.

There were two or three drawings of police controlling the crowds at the Silver Jubilee celebrations in 1935.

[*Punch*, May 1, 1935

1936, the year of the Abdication, also saw the burning to the ground of the Crystal Palace at Sydenham. (*Punch*, it will be remembered, had invented the name 'the Crystal Palace' at the time of the Great Exhibition of 1851. Among the exhibits then displayed had been a patent fire-extinguisher; and the attached notice 'In use at the Exhibition' had led *Punch* to comment: 'We have never heard of the Crystal Palace catching fire!')

The work of the police at the Coronation of 1937 was recognised in *Punch* mainly by humorous drawings of them controlling crowds, with the inevitable lost child.

'PLEASE, CONSTABLE, I'M LOST, AND MOTHER SAYS WOULD YOU PLEASE
PUT ME ON YOUR SHOULDER WHEN THE PROCESSION COMES ALONG?'

[*Punch*, April 28, 1937

It was in 1937 and 1938 that half-a-dozen articles by a new correspondent appeared in the form of parodies of Reports by a detective constable. In the first, Detective Mangle, who has been instructed to inspect theatres, 'respectively reports':

'The manager said I have just recd. a telephone call from a lady who reports that she is proceeding here to shoot me, it is a mercy you are here to arrest her. I immediately replied, Is she in possession of a Gun Licence, & he said Yes, what has that got to do with it. I then said, I cannot arrest this lady for allegedly saying what you allege she allegedly said, it is a Civil Action. . . . Has this lady by word of mouth, written statement or other overt act caused your staff to have a reasonable doubt that a Bch. of Peace is abt. to be committed. He said, No she is too smart for that, & I replied Well, how do they know. . . . I am of the opinion, Sir, that this play is suitable for adult audiences.'

In another, he is sent to investigate larceny of the takings at an art exhibition. Asked what he knows about Neo Vortical Surrealism, he replies without hesitation: 'There is no such offence unless it comes under the Road Transport Lighting Act 1927.' In due course, while effecting arrest of a carpenter for obstructing him while he was trying to remove a window-frame for examination for finger-prints, a pot of glue falls upside down on his plans of the site; and he learns next day that he was being awarded 1st Prize by the Neo Vortical Surrealist Society for a composition entitled 'Shy Violets, Nocturne in Scarlet and Glue'.

Most of his troubles arise, however, in trying to get a car from the sergeant in charge of the police garage.

'I produced signed Order for car, and he said There is only 8 cars in, & I have got to see what is the matter with their insides, you are not going to get any car. I said a Det. is senior to a uniform Sgt, so kindly take instructions from self. He said, You get out of my Garage. I then said, Such refusal will be reported officially by self.'

Police readers will recognise inside knowledge of the Service, even if the general picture is that of the conventional comic stage policeman in those pre-war days. It is a pity that the author, who wrote—I understand—from a police address in Australia, never sent any further articles.

The existence of the women police was at last occasionally recognised by *Punch*—but only incidentally. There was a picture, for instance, of small ragamuffins, one of whom says braggingly: 'The worst o' these women police is yer can't 'it 'em!'; while 'From Our Postbag' there was a letter asking:

' "Can a young man who has become annoyed beyond measure with the police-woman to whom he is engaged to be married be arrested by her for giving her a good smacking on her beat?"

(Ed.—She cannot take him any further into custody. She should untiringly ask him why he is doing it.)'

REHEARSING THE
WESTMINSTER PANTOMIME
P.C. Montague. 'WHAT'S THIS FOR? TO THROW IN THE PUBLIC'S EYES?'
[*Punch*, Dec. 8, 1937

Recruiting for Civil Defence had been in full swing more than a year before the Munich crisis. *Punch* had cartoons appealing for volunteers for the various services, including a police war reserve and Special Constabulary, and many drawings in which domestic life was becoming tangled up with gas-masks, sandbags, air-raid shelters or evacuation camps.

A full-page cartoon by Bernard Partridge in July 1939 showed Sir Samuel Hoare (then Home Secretary) in policeman's uniform about to deal with an I.R.A. man with a truncheon, labelled 'Prevention of Violence Bill'. 'Toby M.P.' reports:

'From rather ludicrous beginnings, in which whitefaced young thugs scattered suitcases full of alarm-clocks which failed to go off, it has become genuinely menacing; the Houses of Parliament have been threatened, and the key documents, which had been seized, included instructions for damaging water-supplies, drainage and the electric grid. The police had been wonderful, but they were badly handicapped without the powers for which he was asking, which extend the right of search and authorise deportation. The opposition remained unhappy about the infringement of liberties; but two nights later, when a bad explosion had just taken place at King's Cross, the Bill passed its Third Reading without a division.'

About this time, many police forces dropped an inch or so off the minimum height at which they would accept recruits. On press reports that examinations by police surgeons in an enquiry for the Home Office had revealed the fact that weight and height are no criterions of strength and efficiency, there were some verses by Jan Struther, 'The Song of the Tiddler':

'The surgeons who picked 'em
Have published this dictum:
"The smallest policemen are often the best";
And I wish to point out
That beyond any doubt
What's true of policemen is true of the rest.'

Recruits for the police force may in future be an inch shorter than formerly. Grateful football spectators are now wondering if there's any chance of their becoming less opaque as well.

[*Punch*, Jan. 26, 1938

CHAPTER VI

The Police and the Public today

*P*unch of 6th September 1939 had gone to press before it was known that we were at war. 'No sops accepted' said a notice board above the Three-headed Watchdog in the Parliamentary cartoon; but 'Charivaria' opened: 'A fine summer is promised for 1940.'

By the following week, Mr Punch was expressing the wish that the sound of cars accelerating in bottom gear bore a less sinister resemblance to the opening note of sirens.

E. V. Knox, who had succeeded Owen Seaman as editor in 1932, continued to hold the post until the end of the war and after. There were nostalgic reproductions of cartoons and pictures from the 1914–1918 war; but for the first six months and more—the period known as 'the phoney war'—*Punch* seems to have tried as far as possible to go on as if nothing had basically changed, the artists doing their best to take the sting out of grim happenings.

'BUT APART FROM THIS, LIFE IS GOING ON JUST THE SAME AS USUAL.'
[*Punch*, Sept. 13, 1939

Hitler's moustache and the Nazi salute were always funny, of course; there were the funny aspects of evacuated town children's reactions to country life; sandbags, the box respirator, and the 'blimps' (or captive barrage balloons) inspired humorous drawings, while ration books and petrol coupons touched *Punch* readers very near home.

'I *CAN'T* MOVE ON—I'VE USED UP ALL MY UNITS.'
[*Punch*, Oct. 18, 1939

In January 1940, 'Dum-Dum' had some verses, 'Gravity in Blue', based on a news item that men of a certain police Division had been instructed not to laugh when on duty.

'Don't try puns on a policeman,
    Don't cheek the gentleman in blue,
        Or you'll run against a snag
        In his loathing of a wag,
    Which is just the sort of thing you shouldn't do;
Don't, when he regulates the traffic,
    Think that it's the moment for a joke,
        For, however near the knuckle,
        He's been told he's not to chuckle,
    And you'll end by being sorry that you spoke.'

A 'tin hat' now replaced the familiar police helmet.

The over-issue of 'O.H.M.S.' and other priority windscreen labels certainly gave occasion for joking (three hundred different varieties of special windscreen labels were counted up). As in the 1914 war, there were inevitably frequent pictorial jokes about the

THE DILEMMA
[*Punch*, Nov. 8, 1939]

enforcement of the black-out—the policeman's or the warden's ability to detect from odd angles some minute chink of light leaking out between curtains, or the pedestrian's nocturnal blunderings by the light of an electric torch covered (as the regulations stipulated) with two thicknesses of tissue paper.

> 'The main cause of accidents', 'Toby M.P.' reported, 'was the fact that pedestrians were alone in being unlighted; but there were difficulties in the way of lighting them.'

(Criminals, too, took time to adjust themselves to the black-out, and an immediate drop in the crime figures had been observed in September.) But the *Punch Almanac for 1940* might almost have been prepared in peace time: perhaps it had been?

By May 1940, jokes on the Home Front became a little more grim, but consistently optimistic. Now the routine of domestic life was upset by the activities of paterfamilias

'I'LL JUST NIP DOWNSTAIRS TO THE STREET AND CHECK UP THAT IT *is your* BLACKOUT. DON'T ADJUST IT; LEAVE IT AS IT IS.'
[*Punch*, Nov. 11, 1942]

as member of the Local Defence Volunteers (soon to be renamed the Home Guard). Soon also there were the humours of air-raid shelter life, and the wry philosophical view of air-raid damage. *Punch* had not really much room for the moment for pictures or jokes about the police, though they were kept busy enough.

> 'The ordinary citizen, suddenly faced with a state of affairs against which he has made little if any provision in advance', the late Sir Philip Game wrote in his Annual Report as Commissioner of Police in 1940, 'is likely to look round for help, and naturally turns to the familiar police officer. The solution of his troubles may be strictly not in any sense a police affair, but in such times as these the police are not too particular about whose job it is.'

In September 1940 there was a full-page drawing by Bernard Partridge 'The Front Line', showing policeman, fireman and A.R.P. warden fighting the blitz—all wearing similar steel helmets.

If a policeman appeared in *Punch* pictures at all, he generally shared the scene with air-raid wardens and the various civil defence functionaries. Some verses in October 1942 under the title 'Co-ordination' emphasised the point.

> 'The Minister told the Police Chief
>   To watch for fires at night,
> The Chief then told the Super
>   To make things watertight;
> The Super told the Constable
>   To see that things were done,
> The P.C. told the Special
>   To rope in everyone.
> The Special told the Fireman
>   To note the various streets,
> The Fireman told the Warden
>   To organise the beats:
> The Warden told the Old Folk
>   What they would have to do,
> And so who fights the fire-bombs now?
>   Why, grandma—ninety-two!'

There were now auxiliary policemen. Recruitment of men to the regular police had been suspended on the outbreak of war. Those with army or navy reserve obligations had of course rejoined at once, and later many more joined the armed forces, so that, before the war was over, the average age of policemen had risen from 35 to 45. Substantial reinforcement was therefore essential. This had been foreseen ever since Munich, and many thousands had already enrolled and were ready to report for duty in September 1939, either as full-time Special Constables, or as War Reserve Constables.

'HOW EXACTLY DO YOU MEAN "AM I RESPONSIBLE FOR THIS INCIDENT"?'

[*Punch*, Jan. 27, 1943

Many of the younger of these subsequently passed into the armed forces, or went off into essential industry; but in the early days they were of all ages, shapes and sizes.

'I'VE ALWAYS WANTED TO BE A POLICEMAN EVER SINCE I WAS SO HIGH.'

[*Punch*, April 16, 1941

Some verses, under the title 'Temporal Power', were to appear in *Punch*.

'Down Whitehall way where the great ones fare,
    Where the cars of Marshals and Sea Lords ply,
At a sight most amazing I stopped to stare:
    A cop with a monocle fixed in his eye.

Old London has lived through her "Finest Hour",
    Her head is erect and her heart remains high,
But she bows with a smile to the temporal power
    Of an eye-glass fixed in a constable's eye.'

Maybe some of them found it difficult to forget their private occupations—though the artist was doubtless letting his imagination run away with himself a bit, in a drawing which appeared in November 1942.

'MIND YOU, THIS IS ONLY A PART-TIME JOB WITH ME.'
[*Punch*, Nov. 11, 1942

(*Punch* of earlier days would not have left you to work out the point for yourself. The caption under the picture would have been somewhat fuller, and might well have read:

'Ex-burglar (who has decided, now that employment as a special constable attracts payment, and the authorities are not too particular about character enquiries, he might as well earn a regular weekly wage):
"The boot's on the other foot now."
Ex-clerk is finding the work hard on his own feet, but being a bit short-sighted, does not like to ask his colleague why he is wearing a mask.')

The Home Secretary was now Mr Herbert Morrison, son of a police constable; and *Punch* twice recorded in their 'Impressions of Parliament' (as 'The Diary of Toby M.P.' was now renamed)—once on a debate on the temporary amalgamation of certain police forces, and again over the release of Sir Oswald Mosley after three years' detention under the Defence Regulations—

'The House rather likes Mr Morrison's forthright way of saying "Move Along there, please." '

War-time red-tape was an obvious target for satire. There was one drawing in a series by Fougasse in 1943, 'The Changing Temper of Britain', which shows a country policeman stopping a car and, instead of asking merely to see the driving licence, he asks:

'May I see your driving licence, please, and your petrol permit and your insurance certificate and your identity cards and your authority for employment of a mechanical vehicle, and your area passes, and your registration book, and the name of your employer, and documents setting forth the nature of employment and reason for which journey undertaken?'

Punch drawings in 1944 dealt largely with jokes about meat, butter, sugar and fuel rationing, clothing coupons and book salvage. But there was a letter about the renewal of an Identity Card which purported to have been signed

'for Chief of Borough Police, by Tempy Resident Representative of Civic Law, now Assistant Adviser to Borough Constabulary, in absence of Chief Inspector, C.I.D., at present engaged in Home Guard duties'.

Red-tape was to continue a subject for criticism after the war was ended. In 1946, for instance, A.P.H. had some verses:

'I want a permit
To ask for a licence
To make application
For a nice fat form.'

It may have been the shortage of petrol that inspired Emett to his picture of the horse-drawn 'Flying Squad'.

'THE FLYING SQUAD, YOUR GRACE.'

[*Punch*, Feb. 24, 1943

Fresh varieties of Service police were now to be seen anywhere and everywhere. One *Punch Almanac* was to show a 'civilian' police constable indignantly looking in through the kitchen window, to see a military policeman getting served by the cook with his traditional rabbit-pie and beer. But it was after America came into the war and American forces were stationed in England that the 'Snowballs' became an even more familiar sight than the 'Red-caps'. A dialogue in *Punch* showed a Londoner trying to show an American soldier round.

'There are one or two places I could show you, but in case they have all been taken over by the Allied Forces, I will just ask a constable.'

The American appeared perplexed.
'A what?'
'You have heard about our famous London police?'
'See here, buddy, we brought our own!'

And another Londoner, in a Fougasse drawing, making conversation with a member of one of the overseas forces, asks:

'And what are your first impressions of our city?'
'I think our policemen are wonderful.'

'Now, HAVE YOU EACH GOT *your* IDENTITY CARD, IN CASE SOME-
ONE IN THERE STARTS GETTING TECHNICAL?'
[*Punch*, Aug. 16, 1944

Punch marked the end of the war with a paragraph in July 1945:

'Next year's Boat-Race will be over the pre-war course, the old Putney–Mortlake–Piccadilly Circus–Vine Street route.'

Things which stood out in daily life at home in 1946 were a post-war crime wave, with hold-ups and smash-and-grab raids by armed bandits, and of course the black market. 'Charivaria' had a paragraph:

'We understand that the object of a recent police comb-out was to detect soldiers with forged military papers, who had deserted from civilian life for the rations.'

In August 1947, following advice on the B.B.C. to householders to co-operate with the police by letting them know when they were going away, but not to leave notices to milkmen, bakers or newspaper boys on the door, there was an article which told how one family had posted the notices to the police, and stuck the note to the police on the door. What really annoyed them was that, while *their* flat was burgled, a neighbour who had left all his windows open when he went away, escaped—the burglars presumably deciding that he must be in residence. A drawing showed a burglar calling at the police station to notify them that *he* was going to be away on holiday for a fortnight.

1947 saw permission given for policemen to wear open collars and ties, instead of the previously regulation upright collar tunic. 'Dum-Dum' had some verses:

'He moves among us austere and grave,
   A stiffened and a stark reproof
To those with a leaning to misbehave,
   Majestic, unlike, aloof.

But loosen him up with collar and tie,
   A man among other men,
The awe may lessen, the reverence die,
   And where should we all be then?'

'TCH! TCH! I'VE BEEN DOING NOTHING ELSE ALL MORNING.'
[*Punch*, Aug. 23, 1950

In 'Essence of Parliament', an M.P. is reported as having said that the bald heads of so many policemen were due to their having to wear helmets; and a sympathetic drawing of two elderly station officers demonstrated the obverse side of what a character in one of Somerset Maugham's early comedies had said:

> 'The first sign of old age is when you go out into the streets of London and realise for the first time how young the policemen look.'

'EVER NOTICE HOW ALL THE CRIMINALS SEEM TO LOOK YOUNGER NOWADAYS?'
[*Punch*, June 29, 1950

Most police forces, especially those in London and the large provincial cities, were at this time well below establishment figures, having never overtaken their post-war deficiencies. Not all those who had been seconded to the armed forces returned, after having risen in the commissioned ranks. Of the London police alone, nearly 500 were killed on active service abroad, while over 200 lost their lives on duty in air raids. Many elderly policemen who had stayed on were overdue for retirement. In spite of the improvements now given in pay and general conditions of service, the recruiting position was still a cause of anxiety a few years later, when a full-page cartoon by Illingworth showed queues for National Service outside a recruiting depot for the Navy, Army or Air Force, with a police sergeant outside the adjoining police station saying:

17

'Why can't some of them come over here—and help to defend the homes they're leaving?'

'Charivaria' in July 1954, commenting on a proposal in one county that roads would be patrolled by policemen in plain clothes, notices being erected announcing the fact, said:

'Nothing could be more firmly in line with the British tradition of fair play— unless the authorities feel that they could go one better and admit that there aren't any policemen—just the notice.'

The Lynskey Tribunal in 1948 was the subject of more than one cartoon; but there were no pictures or notes referring to the background to the setting up in the same year under Lord Oaksey of a Committee on Police Conditions of Service, nor of the House of Commons' reception of that Committee's Report a year later, reassessing the status of the policeman in terms of remuneration, besides introducing for the first time a 'London Allowance'. A general review of current problems did however include a hypothetical account of a policeman's dissatisfaction with the stipulation that it would be necessary to go on serving another three years to get the higher pensions, which were now to be based on averaging. 'The necessary increase in the numbers of the Force,' he is supposed to have added, 'would never be achieved unless all the men in it could retire at once.'

The film *The Blue Lamp*, shown in 1950, had been made with a good deal of co-operation from Scotland Yard. It introduced Dixon, the solid, reliable and very human middle-aged constable at Dock Green; and there was a cartoon in *Punch* of the principal characters.

[*The Blue Lamp*

BAD HATS AND GOOD

Riley—DIRK BOGARDE; *Spud*—PATRIC DOONAN; *P.C. Mitchell*—JIMMY HANLEY; *P.C. Dixon*—JACK WARNER

[*Punch*, Feb. 1, 1950

Punch now began to pay more attention to the women police—who since the war were to be seen in the streets in considerably increasing numbers, both in London and in most provincial towns—though his artists seemed always to see them with the same long pointed or bulbous noses as they saw policemen or indeed anyone else. (In a drawing of an identity parade in June 1958, the nose is really the only thing the people in the line have in common.) Douglas was responsible for most of the drawings of women police in the 'fifties. There were two of women in uniform dallying to look in shop windows, and tempted by a hat. There was one of a policewoman sitting on a jewel thief and pausing to study the Judo instruction book. And Norman Mansbridge had one of a policewoman glued interminably to the telephone, while four policemen waited impatiently in a queue to take their turns.

[*Punch*, Nov. 29, 1950

Douglas had a strip cartoon of one turning a girl off a park seat where she is being cuddled by a man—and then taking her place. In another, she is shown in the park arresting Cupid and taking his bow and arrow away. But wearing a uniform, a woman remains a woman: policewomen have even been known to marry policemen.

[*Punch*, Jan. 14, 1959

There was a picture by Larry in 1958 of a policewoman directing traffic with her handbag slung from her wrist; and the agenda of 'Cops in Conclave' in 1950 included the item: 'Should mounted policewomen ride side-saddle?'

There were still mounted police, and pictures of them appeared from time to time. In one, in 1956, a crook is shown offering the horse sugar, while his accomplice carries out a hold-up at a jewellers' just round the corner. In 'Impressions of Parliament' in February 1955, the Home Secretary, asked why mounted police had been used against demonstrators in Parliament Square, is reported to have forborne from making the obvious point that, if mounted police exacerbate crowds, it is because they bring them under police control. This is accompanied by a small cartoon of Major Lloyd George, in police uniform on a horse, trampling on Aneurin Bevan and Ben Parkin.

The motor-car and the traffic problem naturally form subjects for pictures or articles almost every week. A.P.H. had put the revised Highway Code of 1946 into verse. In 1952 there was a full page of drawings 'At the Cross-Roads' by E. V. Shepard, which showed the police constable as an orchestral conductor, and some verses by Mark Bevan:

> 'Aloof, impartial 'mid the roll
> Of traffic's tympani and horn,
> High on his rostrum in control—
> The constable conducts each morn.
>
> O Sargent! of the rank P.C.,
> O Boult! from out the men in blue,
> Some brighter beat (it seems to me)
> Some better baton's due to you.'

Inevitably it is the *contretemps* of the private motorist which inspire pictures almost every week. In 1948, while the restrictions of basic petrol prevailed, there was a full-page drawing by Illingworth, showing the inoffensive little family motorist being harassed by policemen, Ministry of Fuel officials, A.A. Scouts and Sherlock Holmes himself, to make sure whether he was not committing some offence.

HEY FOR THE OPEN ROAD!

[*Punch*, May 19, 1948

E. S. Turner, in an article several years later, 'The Shape of Crimes to Come', imagines the case of a motorist being fined £5 for driving away from a car park without tipping the attendant, being under the impression (from which the chairman of the bench quickly and contemptuously disabuses his mind) that free car parks were free. Another defendant at the same court is sentenced, under a new Road Courtesy Act, to seven days for having failed to make a 'sign, signal, movement or gesture indicative of appreciation or obligement' to a motorist who allowed him to use a pedestrian crossing. Suggestions for segregation of pedestrians and vehicular traffic were to lead *Punch* to ask: 'Should mixed marriages between motorists and pedestrians be forbidden by law?'

In 1952 Illingworth had another full-page cartoon, entitled simply 'Central London', which shows two distraught police constables carrying 'No Waiting' notices, and being asked by John Bull, who brings another notice board inscribed 'No Private Cars in this area without a permit', 'Have you ever thought of trying something like this?'

There were frequent pictures showing private cars which had been left immediately under 'No Waiting' notices. The proposal to introduce parking meters on the American plan is first mentioned in a paragraph in 'Charivaria' in 1953; and they appear thereafter from time to time in pictures; the illegally parked car being towed away by the police does not appear until 1958.

The Street Crossing Patrols first appear in a drawing in 1954. The 'L plate' naturally cropped up from time to time as a subject upon which to hang a joke. It appears, as recently as 1962, as fore and aft decoration on a dapple-grey horse being ridden up to Westminster, which inspires *Punch* to question whether horse and rider ought to travel as a pedestrian or a vehicle. (The question also arises whether the 'L plates' ought to be worn by the horse or the rider.)

In 1956 there was a cartoon of the Minister of Transport in police uniform, hung about with placards—'Road Closed', 'No Thoroughfare', 'Road Up', 'No Entry', 'Danger Diversion', 'Slow'. Another full-page drawing was to show the motorist on the open road, completely distracted by having to look at so many different traffic signs.

The advantages of automatic traffic signals had their limitations: there was a full-page cartoon by Hickey, which showed a constable surrounded by jammed cars at a cross-roads with automatic light signals at each corner, and saying:

> 'I don't know why you're worrying about automation. It hasn't put *me* out of a job.'

The question of the interpretation of 'in charge of a car' in connection with drink was also being much discussed in Parliament and elsewhere. In August 1955 *Punch* had a drawing of a car, drawn half across the verge, displaying a notice:

> 'Inebriated but not in charge: PLEASE PASS.'

E. S. Turner's 'Crimes to Come' include being in charge of a motor vehicle while under the influence of *food*. The accused, found at the wheel in a state of complete collapse, admits having eaten a seven-course dinner on top of a six-course luncheon, with a number of snacks in between. Asked by the Chairman how much alcohol he had had to drink, he replies that he is a teetotaller. The Chairman, putting him on probation for a year, says: 'A man in your position ought to know that it is extremely dangerous to consume large quantities of food without benefit of alcohol.'

There is a picture in January 1960 of two jovial policemen, helping an obviously intoxicated man out of the driving seat and saying:

'Fair's fair. If you pass the alcohol test, we'll buy you a drink.'

In August 1963 in an article 'The New Drinkers', based on the Home Secretary's decision to have an enquiry into drink offences, various imaginary police court hearings are reported. In one, a middle-aged man wearing an R.A.C. tie is charged with attempting to commit suicide, with a parking-meter strung round his neck, his breath smelling strongly of alcohol. His counsel says:

'For the past twelve months, my client has spent his waking life driving between meter-spaces in Central London—every hour, on the hour. As a direct result, his business has collapsed, and his liver has sustained permanent disability.'

Learning that he has had a previous conviction for inflicting Actual Bodily Harm on a parking-attendant while under the influence, the magistrate remands him for a psychiatrist's report.

The raising of the speed limit in certain areas from 30 to 40 m.p.h. in 1960 produced a picture of a motorist stopped for exceeding the new limit and protesting:

'You know perfectly well I always went through it at 40 when it said 30, so why shouldn't I go through it at 50 when it says 40?'

And a note in 'Charivaria', commenting on an announcement by the Minister of Works that the speed limit in the Royal Parks was being raised from 20 to 30 m.p.h. 'as the best way to get respect for the law', says:

'This seems a new line in jurisprudence: the legislator should find out what people do and then make it legal. An increase of convictions for any crime would presumably be a reason for removing it from the calendar.'

Policemen as motorists—whether as traffic patrols or in squad cars—naturally find their way into pictures from time to time; and the increasing use of motor-cycles or scooters by constables patrolling on outlying beats inspired at least one humorous drawing.

'AT LEAST THIS PUTS AN END TO HIS "OH, MY POOR FEET!"'

[*Punch*, July 6, 1955

In the 'fifties, under the editorships of Kenneth Bird (1949–52) and Malcolm Muggeridge (1953–57), *Punch* shed much of its Edwardian make-up, and became more topical and satirical, with quite serious feature articles on current social problems. There were 'The New Mayhew', for instance, Claud Cockburn's 'Aspects of English History', Geoffrey Gorer's 'Modern Types', and some purely factual articles by writers like G. W. Stonier, John Betjeman and Patrick Balfour (Lord Kinross). There were special numbers covering some particular subject—none, so far, up to the time of writing, about the police—and regular columns 'In the City', 'In the Country', two pages expressly for women, and competitions. P. G. Wodehouse came back after nearly fifty years to contribute a frequent 'Letter from New York'.

The policeman figures less frequently nowadays in drawings or verse than he used to. The new type coming out of the Hendon Police College had offered a subject for many gentle digs in the 'thirties; the opening and development of a National Police College after the war has passed almost unnoticed by *Punch*. So did the loss by forty-five large towns of their separate police forces in 1947. The policeman on duty among the crowds used to be a frequent figure in humorous drawings at the time of the Great Exhibition of 1851, and at Jubilees or Coronations; he does not appear at all in Mr Punch's special numbers for the Festival of Britain in 1951 or Queen Elizabeth II's coronation in 1953.

There were of course references here and there. 'A political policeman's lot is decidedly not a happy one', Malcolm Muggeridge wrote in an article on the downfall of Beria in 1953, following Stalin's death; and Senator McCarthy's report on un-American activities did not go unnoticed in 1954. That year the very detailed provisions of a new Protection of Birds Act inspired H. F. Ellis to an article 'The Policeman at Nesting Time', in which he points out that all officers will now have to familiarise themselves with the distinctive colouration and markings of the eggs of all birds on the list, in order to avoid wrongful arrest for behaving in a manner calculated to harass and annoy brooding or expectant birds. Constable Boot reappears in a Misleading Case in 1955, giving evidence of the arrest of Albert Haddock for brawling in church; his grounds of appeal from his conviction under an Act of 1860 are that he had felt impelled to take the opportunity, in giving his daughter away, of protesting at the small recognition given to the important role of the bride's father. In 'Essence of Parliament' that year there are two cartoons of politicians in police uniform—Major Lloyd George, as Home Secretary, giving the Government's reasons for turning down the recommendations of the Gowers Committee on capital punishment; and Mr Chuter Ede, an ex-Home Secretary, protecting Major Lloyd George when a Bill about horror-comics was under discussion.

The Soho Fair of 1956, which followed shortly after a series of razor-slashing cases, was the subject of two pages of drawings by Sprod in the issue of July 4th.

A GAME OF BLIND MAN'S BLUFF

[*Punch*, July 4, 1956

The one reproduced here would have become less apposite after the passing of the Street Offences Act of 1959, which inspired a drawing by Bernard Hollowood of an elderly woman in foggy weather by a bus stop saying plaintively to a P.C:

> 'I've been waiting for a No. 9 Bus for two hours and been cautioned five times!'

In July 1957, when the ethics of 'telephone tapping' were arousing some concern, there was one drawing of a good-looking young detective sergeant calling on a film star, having overheard that she had not got a date that evening.

On a debate in the Commons in June 1960 on a private member's motion on the Wolfenden Report, *Punch*'s Parliamentary correspondent sums up:

> 'The general view of the House seemed to be that the present law is idiotic but on no account to be changed. Mr Butler was clearly anxious not to be saddled, as he was over capital punishment, with a half-responsibility for giving facilities for a Bill which most of his own supporters did not like. He therefore characteristically offered the reformers everything except help.'

Crime is naturally the topic with which police are most obviously concerned; and the victim of burglars is an easy subject for humour—just as the man slipping up on a banana skin has always been.

Anton's drawings of masked burglars, spivs and forgers appeared frequently.

'Impressions of Parliament' in 1948 had been full of the debates on the Criminal Justice Bill of that year, which was to abolish corporal punishment and introduce Preventive Detention. (Sales of copies of the Act, it is said, were brisk among experienced crooks, who wanted to know exactly where they stood.) A clause suspending the death penalty for an experimental period of five years was passed by the Commons, but was thrown out by the House of Lords, where, *Punch* noted, Judges and ex-Home Secretaries were almost unanimous in opposing it. Meanwhile 'A.P.H.' in the Misleading Case of *Rex* v. *Bopple* had made the Judge say, in his summing up to the jury:

> 'If you find the prisoner guilty, it will be my duty formally to pass sentence of death upon him according to law. But it is as certain as anything can be that that sentence will not be carried out. . . . The prisoner, it may be, has not many years to live. It is likely that, in many ways, he would live those years more comfortably in prison than he would outside. He would be housed, fed, clothed and doctored by the State, with none of the troubles of rent, repairs, rates and taxes, ration-books and coupons and insurance payments which beset the free man. Many a lonely old man might envy him.'

The jury, after a few minutes' deliberation, found the prisoner 'Not Guilty'. The prisoner scowled angrily, and said:

> 'That was a dirty trick, my Lord. I thought I had everything in the bag.'

When the Homicide Act of 1957 came to be discussed, *Punch* in 'Essence of Parliament' sums the Bill up as a political compromise between a House of Commons that is abolitionist and a House of Lords and a Government that are anti-abolitionist—a race to get the Government's Bill through the House before Mr Silverman's resurrected total abolition Bill could be brought in. In the Lords, it is commented that the Archbishop of Canterbury's hope that this measure will end the controversy, at least for the time being, looks as if it will be singularly unlikely to be fulfilled.

At the time of the Bournemouth East by-election in January 1959, *Punch* prints an alleged telegram to the Local Conservative Association, which includes:

> 'Favour flogging unless it brutalises in which case substitute capital punishment provided not carried out during lifetime of offender.'

Psychoanalysis was even more fashionable than it had been before the war; and the psychiatrist's couch appears frequently in *Punch* drawings. Evoe had some verses in April 1950 on its application to the juvenile delinquent.

> 'Tom, Tom, the piper's son
>   Stole a pig and away he run.
> The pig was missed, and Tom was kissed
>   And sent to a psychiatrist!'

The psychiatrist's report to the magistrate runs:

> 'The little mind is split
> But we must make the best of it;
> Subliminal desire for pork
> Is often much too hard to balk,
> And in some cases may extrude
> The sense of moral turpitude;
> Complete dispersal of the former
> Should metagrobolise the Trauma.
>
> The beak, at once impressed by this
> Superbly phrased analysis,
>   Dispatched to a Remedial Home
>   The adolescent gastronome.
> Here he forgot that ancient sin
> For which the cops had pulled him in,
>   And nothing in his mind was left
>   Associating "pigs" with "theft".'

In a 'Dramatic Fragment "Cops in Conclave"' about the same time, R. G. G. Price makes a Superintendent point out that welfare work was blunting the use of coppers' narks, who tended more and more to resort to milk bars and public libraries,

where they learned less of what went on. The same author had another article in
October 1951, 'The Psychological Sleuth'.

> 'Within a few minutes of the body's being discovered, The Yard was on the way.
> The prowl car was followed by the encephalograph van, the schizophrenia squad and
> the couches for witnesses—interviewing. . . . The C.I.D. man had the best record in
> Homicide—never charged a man who had not ended in Broadmoor. . . . His younger
> colleagues found the Superintendent's old-fashioned approach galling at times: he
> had read no psychology later than William James.'

The development of the 'Identikit', synchronising with more than one case of thefts
of pictures, led *Punch* in 1962 to suggest a new Art Squad with 'A-Cars', who would be
able to make a mock-up of the next stolen portrait.

There was nothing new about juvenile crime, though it had become more prominent
since the war. This has been variously attributed to absence of parental influence, the
Welfare State, the films and television. As far back as 1946 'Charivaria' had a note:

> 'There have been so many armed hold-ups and smash-and-grab raids recently
> that magistrates are expected to compel juvenile delinquents to go to the cinema so
> that they may not be influenced by what goes on outside.'

The Teddy Boy first appears in a *Punch* picture in 1954. In July 1956 there is a picture of one being interrogated by a police constable and explaining the reason why he
is laid out:

> 'My bicycle chain broke.'

Punch like the press generally could but comment from time to time on the mounting
numbers of serious crimes, including offences of violence, at a time when the nation was
never more prosperous and social conditions never better. In September 1956 they had
a four-page inset, 'The British Cracksman (incorporating "Felon's Gazette" and
"Weekly Con-Man")' and in November 1959 there was a two-page illustrated article
'How to breast the Crime Wave'.

Everyone recognised that the police were suffering from inadequate numbers; only
increased co-ordination and pooling of resources helped to counteract this.

Organised crimes such as pay-roll robberies and the holding-up of banks and post
offices, often with firearms, were reaching new proportions. In 1955 A.P.H. had had
some verses, commenting on the way people always seem to do what they are told, when
a pistol is levelled at them, even though the chances are that the criminal may be as
nervous as they are.

> 'I hope that when the next young tough
>   Says "It's a stick-up—see?"
> Some citizen will call the bluff
>   (Though it may not be me.)'

'HE ISN'T IN; COULD I TAKE A MESSAGE?'

[*Punch*, May 20, 1953

In the same year, there had been a picture of a P.C. taking particulars from a motorist for leaving his car by a 'No Waiting' notice outside a Bank, and saying to him: 'Sorry, didn't hear your name on account of that gelignite explosion.'

Privately-run organisations, on the lines of those which had already existed in other countries, providing armoured vans with uniformed guards as escorts for the collection and delivery of wages or other valuables, were however beginning to attract the attention of *Punch*.

'THESE PARA-MILITARY POLICE ORGANISATIONS ARE BECOMING SOMETHING OF A MENACE.'

[*Punch*, Jan. 16, 1963

A paragraph in 'Charivaria' suggests that the time is coming when our milk-books, grocery-books and laundry-books should carry the item '10% armed robbery surcharge'. Meanwhile however J. B. Boothroyd had suggested in an article that it was about time the press should lump all the robberies into one column headed 'Weekend Raids', thus denying the criminal the added enjoyment of gloating over his headlines, and sparing the ordinary law-abiding reader from stale wading through columns of small type in which reporters strive to gloss the tedium of crime fact with the glamour of crime fiction.

None-the-less, the press aid the police in following up any line which may enable them to trace people who 'they think may be able to help them in their enquiries'.

'WE BELIEVE HE MAY BE ABLE TO HELP US IN OUR INQUIRIES.'
[*Punch*, Feb. 6, 1963

The most pressing problem, said a note in 'Charivaria' in February 1954, was to make crime fiction stranger than fact. It was the hey-day of the detective of fiction, and *Punch* articles cropped up fairly regularly, analysing where he stood in relation to 'the official detective'.

Sherlock Holmes was undying—Evoe in particular went on writing about him in *Punch*—though Inspectors Gregson or Lestrade never seemed to get any credit. The anniversary of the foundation of an Association of British Private Detectives inspired two articles in 1954, contrasting the bucolic florid-faced ex-C.I.D. man who (Geoffrey Lincoln wrote) is usually to be seen in the box giving evidence in the divorce court, with the lean, saturnine-faced Philip Marlowe with his snap-brimmed hat and pistol under his arm-pit—solitary, exhausted, 'the spirit of disillusioned justice', with too many empty hours to drink bourbon or rye in his dusty office. He never seems to sit down to eat a meal (Stella Gibbons points out) without being interrupted in the first mouthful by the telephone or a dame at the door—what a contrast with the amenities enjoyed by Holmes and Watson, Hercule Poirot or Reggie Fortune!

'IT WAS JUST A CASE OF THE PERFECT CRIME CLASHING WITH
THE PERFECT INVESTIGATION.'

[*Punch*, Jan. 16, 1963

Nowadays in crime fiction as often as not the official C.I.D. inspector or superintendent has replaced the inspired amateur; while discharged prisoners publish almost as many volumes of reminiscences as retired C.I.D officers. (The story is told of the literary personage, invited to give a talk on books to prisoners, finding that when she asked at the end of her talk if there were any questions, all they wanted to know was the name of a good literary agent!)

Punch reviews of television programmes included cartoons of Detective Chief Superintendent Lockhart and of Dixon of Dock Green. The influence on juveniles of television stories of crime and violence has been discussed *ad nauseam*. But—as a recent book on juvenile offenders published in the U.S.A. points out—television at least has a better record than the police, for every television law-breaker is brought to justice.

Independent Television started in 1955; and a year later *Punch* gives a warning that, although the number of television licences had passed 6 million, upstairs bedrooms did not necessarily offer soft cribs to ladder-men whilst the family were viewing downstairs: statistics showed (the writer says) that in more and more families, at least one member tended to withdraw from the viewing circle and take refuge in bed.

E. S. Turner's 'Crimes to Come' include the case of a man charged with failing to answer a question put to him in the street by a hatless, unkempt television interviewer who poked him in the stomach with a hand microphone. His defence, that he did not answer because he had not given the matter thought, was regarded as ridiculous and undemocratic. 'How could television programmes be produced if everyone took your attitude?' the magistrate asks—and fines him £2.

In March 1960 there was a picture of a prisoner being interviewed by six police officers—some in plain clothes—and protesting: 'What the hell *is* this? A television interview?' Another shows a TV interviewer having chosen a 'No Waiting' site on which to stop his car in order to get a police sergeant to give his views on car parking.

In 1960 *Punch* decided to imagine a 'Shadow Cabinet' made up of various personages selected by them as suitable to fill the different offices. In a series of articles, the Home Secretaryship naturally went to A.P.H., who wrote:

'My predecessor, Mr R. A. Butler, has stolen much of my ancient thunder.'

After dealing in some detail with what remains outstanding on such matters as Lord's Day Observance and Liquor Licensing, he goes on to say:

'As I said nearly two years ago to the Electors of East Harrow: I am as uneasy as many of you about savage crimes and soft corrections. . . .

I know the arguments against—and I know I shall madden some of the local boys. But I *think* I shall try to bring all the police under my wing. It is absurd that the conduct of the police can only be discussed in Parliament if my dear Metropolitans are concerned. Thus, too, I shall be better able to pet the police as I should like to, and get them lots of pay.'

Although, he says, he may not go quite so far as his 'Spring (Arrangements) Bill' which he drafted in verse in 1936,

'All my heads of departments will have to wear carnations, and at lunch-time a band will play in the Home Office hall.'

Mr Punch as a policeman—his cloak covering a whole variety of stray dogs, led by Toby—monopolised the coloured cover for 14th October 1959. That year, a few controversial cases had left the police in one of their periodical bad patches, so far as the newspapers and public gossip were concerned. There were debates in the House, and Mr R. A. Butler the Home Secretary announced that he had decided to set up a Royal Commission. There was a full-page cartoon by Norman Mansbridge.

'. . . AND NOW—ABOUT YOUR RELATIONS WITH THE PUBLIC.'

[*Punch*, Dec. 2, 1959

C. H. Rolph, a retired police officer of some seniority, whose writings on police and criminal matters carry considerable weight, had a long article in *Punch* of 2nd December, 'Who is Pushing Who Around?' (arising from a remark by printing strikers: 'Push the coppers off the street!')

> 'Are we afraid of the police? We approach them, if we must, with a sickly grin of ingratiation. We have a special way of going into a police station to make even the most innocuous enquiry. If the Station Officer is brusque, we are prepared to come out and write an anonymous letter to the papers . . . How much are the police part of ourselves? Not much. There is no longer any substance in the notion that they are merely plain citizens doing for payment what we could all legally be required to do for nothing: it went out with the Parish Constable and the paid deputy. But because of their ancient origin, the piecemeal growth of their job, and the British preference for an unwritten Constitution, they enjoy (or exercise) enormous scope for initiative, the Blind Eye or the Deaf Ear. Never has Parliament prescribed their limitations; instead it has subjected them to numerous penalties for neglect of duty, i.e. not pushing hard enough . . . The novel, the film, the theatre and television authors rely partly on each other and partly on what the police are prepared to tell them when they are "getting their facts". They all accordingly portray the English policeman as a staccato despot in a raincoat . . . Even old George Dixon (of Dock Green) chances his arm, without knowing what he is chancing, getting away every Saturday evening with the constabulary equivalent of murder. . . .
>
> There are young policemen who enforce regulations which most people consider pettifogging, because they have not yet understood the English passion for making regulations which are not on any account to be enforced. It is the older constables, the George Dixons, who bluff. There remain the minority who lose their tempers, a catastrophically easy thing to do on police duty. . . . The modern citizen needs to keep a wary eye on the police machine; but the machine runs better on oil than it does on grit.'

The Royal Warrant appointing the Commission was signed in January 1960, with wide terms of reference to review the constitutional position of the police throughout Great Britain, and the arrangements for their control and administration—with particular attention to their relationship with the public. It was decided that the most urgent matter, if recruits with the proper qualifications were to be attracted and retained, was to settle the principles which should govern the pay status of the lower ranks; and an interim report dealing with this was presented and accepted by the government before the end of the year. Salary scales were now substantially raised. The Commission's final report did not come out until May 1962: having listened to much evidence from all sides, they were clear that nothing had gone fundamentally wrong between the police and the public.

The police of necessity live perennially on thin ice. C. H. Rolph collected the views and experiences of a number of people from various professions and occupations, ranging from barristers and police officers to criminals, and published them

'SHOULD AULD ACQUAINTANCE BE FORGOT . . .'

[*Punch*, Dec. 30, 1959

in 1962 in a book *The Police & The Public*. Christopher Hollis, reviewing it in *Punch*, wrote:

> 'All the writers seem oppressed with the fact that the policeman is a man apart, looked at by his neighbours as someone different. So he is. But, in different ways, so are the clergyman and the schoolmaster and many others. The policeman is unique —but he is not unique in being unique.
>
> The general conclusion seems to be that police are not very popular but that they never have been. I suspect that this is true and that the main difference between our times and Victorian times is that in Victorian times the classes that had most reason to dislike the police had least facilities for expressing their opinions in print. . . . I do not like boasting criminals. I think things have gone too far when the criminals start saying of us who are more or less law-abiding: "There but for the grace of God go I!" '

A few weeks later there was an article by H. F. Ellis:

> 'Some people just do not like policemen. Myself, I am rather a romanticist about the Force, feeling kindly and a little meek towards them. . . . When I see two of them meet and speak together in the street, I am conscious how far they are set apart from other men by their responsibilities, their special knowledge, their strong bonds of loyalty. I know that if one of them were killed, the other would never rest until his murderers were brought to justice; and this is something I could not say about any other couple I happen to see in the street. In books, I like them to do well, and would always rather follow the investigations of a professional detective than of any tedious amateur, however well-born.'

He goes on to speak of the American police of fiction, whose 'one honest cop per book does not at all reconcile me to those others who only stop assaulting witnesses when they want both hands free to take bribes'.

Of the police of Police States, he writes:

> 'They do not suffer the inconvenience of being attacked, misrepresented and mocked in the literature of their fellow citizens'.

(But according to *Pravda* and *Isvestia*,

> 'If he is not regarded with distaste, the policeman is often ridiculed. Some of our writers, journalists and dramatists have an incorrect attitude towards the policeman, whom they depict tendentiously and in an ugly manner.')

Sprod's New Year's Eve cartoon in 1959 may well have had the recent Street Offences Act as well as the pending Royal Commission in mind.

The Aldermaston marchers and the demands they made on police attention, with its ridiculous sides, gave material for several pictures in *Punch*. There was one in March 1957 by David Langdon, where a policeman on a horse, waiting for the procession to arrive, asks another: 'What's it today? H-Bombs, or Eleven-plus?' Another by him, illustrating the philosophical patience of the police, appeared in March 1961.

'AT LEAST IT KEEPS THEIR CARS OFF THE ROAD.'

[*Punch*, March 29, 1961

There was an article in May 1962, 'How to be a Pressure Group'.

'Unless you tell the police exactly what you hope to do, they will not be able to prevent you. And part of the glorious democratic joy of being a pressure group will be lost. . . . The trouble is, with all this sitting, the police are finding it harder and harder to distinguish one Cause from another. Make sure you get carried away for *your* Cause, and not someone else's.'

There were some verses by J. E. Hinder in February 1963:

'(TUNE: *Villikins and his Dinah*.)
As I was a-walking round *Traf*-algar Square
   I met a young maiden with long matted hair,
A pair of black-wool-stockings, a boilerman's hat
   And a Ban-the-Bomb-Banner at-the-foot-of-which she sat.

I said "Are you married or courting, my dove?"
   She replied "I've not found one who's worthy-of-my-love,
For he must be a Bomb-Banner, against-the-colour-bar,
   Wear a beard, sing Greek folk-songs and play the guitar." '

'CONSTABLE!'

[*Punch*, June 7, 1961

Punch was restrained in its references to the post-Profumo scandals. In August 1963 there was a small drawing by Hollowood of a simple girl kneeling by her bed praying:

'And, please, let the befouled air of my beloved Britain, with its squalid scandals and shabby intrigue, be cleansed by another big, decent mail-train robbery.'

There were a series of articles, 'Morality 1963', in which different writers discussed the Commandments observed and broken in various social fields. C. H. Rolph, in an article 'The Legal Pyramid', lumped policemen with solicitors' and barristers' clerks, Customs officers, park-keepers, railway officials, traffic wardens and coastguards as the 'other ranks' of the law, who, since—with rare and refreshing exceptions—they see only one kind of law coming from only one source, identify themselves with the whole body of it, recognise any set of printed rules as evidence of the *Vox Dei*, and are likely to take any breach as a personal affront.

> 'Policemen's moral lives owe something to a disciplinary concept called "the reputation of the force" and the heinousness of tarnishing this by "bringing discredit on it". This is akin to the military man's pitfall "conduct prejudicial to good order and military discipline". It gives protection to a notional police reputation considerably higher than in cold fact prevailing at any given moment.'

Punch had nothing at all to say, by cartoon, in prose or in verse, on the subject of the Police Bill, introduced in November 1963 by Mr Henry Brooke, now the Home Secretary, to give statutory effect to the principal changes in police administration which the Royal Commission had recommended eighteen months before; nor on points which arose in the final discussions in both Houses of Parliament in the spring of 1964.

The policeman still figures in an occasional humorous drawing, but in most cases merely as up against the motorist. In one, in December 1963, the offending motorist's conventional complaint: 'Wouldn't you be better employed catching burglars?' is varied to: 'Why aren't you protecting the Beatles?'

The growing practice of circulating pamphlets of official admonition and advice— including more than one to householders or motorists on 'How You can Help the Police to Help You'—inspired a parody in *Punch* in October 1963: 'Your Policemen and You' ('How to keep out of the hands of the Police and how to avoid unnecessary discomfort and inconvenience should you be arrested').

> 'Remember that *you* have to pay your policemen, and it is therefore only common sense to keep their numbers down by using them as little as possible. Remember that the cost of cell-cleaning and Black Maria upkeep is a charge on *your* pocket.
>
> Make *quite sure* at all times that you are not in possession of offensive weapons or the property of third parties. Robbery and murder take up as much police time as anything, motoring offences apart.
>
> Arrest *could* occur, and you are advised to have a small bag with overnight necessities ready packed and easily accessible.'

In a recent case under the Obscene Publications Act 1959 the conviction of a man for selling 'filthy pictures' had been quashed 'with some reluctance' by the Court of Criminal Appeal, on the ground that the principal prosecution witnesses, two detective officers to whom the photographs had been sold, were not susceptible of being depraved or corrupted; and this led A. P. Herbert to one more Misleading Case, in which the

Crown appeals to the House of Lords. The Lord Chancellor expresses sympathy with 'the Incorruptible Cops'.

'They move among us as men apart' he is represented as saying, 'neutral and passionless as monks or doctors, as hard to shock as coroners or mortuary officials'.

To which Lord Wool interjects: 'Come off it, Chancellor!', and goes on to give his judgment:

> 'These incorruptible cops don't live in a vacuum. They've got a staff, ain't they? secretaries and so forth—some of these beardless "boy-cops" you see everywhere. I'll bet you some of them took a look at the pretty pictures, and if they ain't corruptible, I'm going to deem they are. The conviction should stand.'

The Crown's appeal was allowed.

Julian Symons, reviewing a book by a young barrister on The Police, published in April 1964, summarises the author's principal suggestions for the future of the police, and concludes:

> 'Shall we then have a perfect police force? By no means. The conflict between the rights of the individual and the rights of society will always go on, and the very existence of the police is an expression of it.'

'THIS IS THE PART I ALWAYS FEEL SHOWS US UP IN A
VERY POOR LIGHT . . .'
[*Punch*, Sept. 24, 1952

PRINTED IN GREAT BRITAIN BY
THE ANCHOR PRESS, TIPTREE